Finland

Finland

BY GERI CLARK

Enchantment of the World™
Second Series

Children's Press®

An Imprint of Scholastic Inc.

NEW YORK TORONTO LONDON AUCKLAND SYDNEY
MEXICO CITY NEW DELHI HONG KONG
DANBURY, CONNECTICUT

Frontispiece: A Sámi girl with a reindeer

Consultant: Jason Lavery, Associate Professor of History, Oklahoma State University

Please note: All statistics are as up-to-date as possible at the time of publication.

Book production by Herman Adler

Library of Congress Cataloging-in-Publication Data

Clark, Geri, 1970–
 Finland / by Geri Clark.
    p. cm. —(Enchantment of the world. Second series)
 Includes bibliographical references and index.
 Summary: This book on Finland explores both historical and cultural
aspects of the European country.
 ISBN-13: 978-0-531-12098-9
 ISBN-10: 0-531-12098-8
 1. Finland—Juvenile literature. [1. Finland.] I. Title. II. Series.
 DL1012.C63 2008
 948.97—dc22   2008000649

Finland

Cover photo:
Children enjoying a
reindeer sled ride

Contents

Olavinlinna Castle

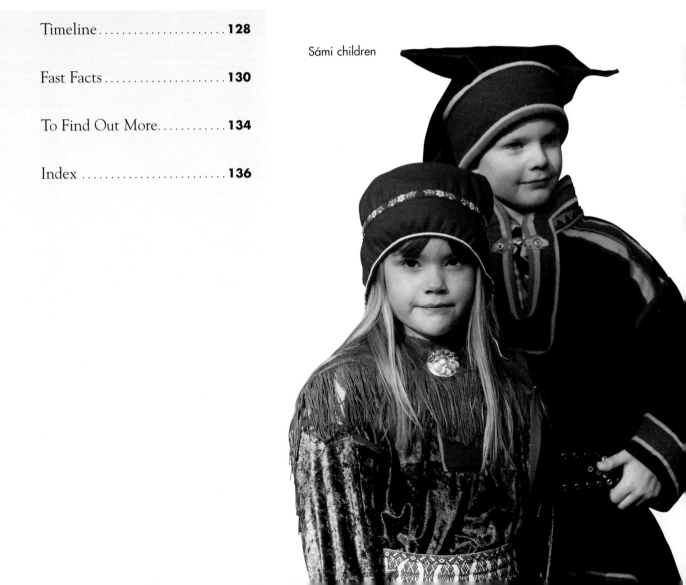

Sámi children

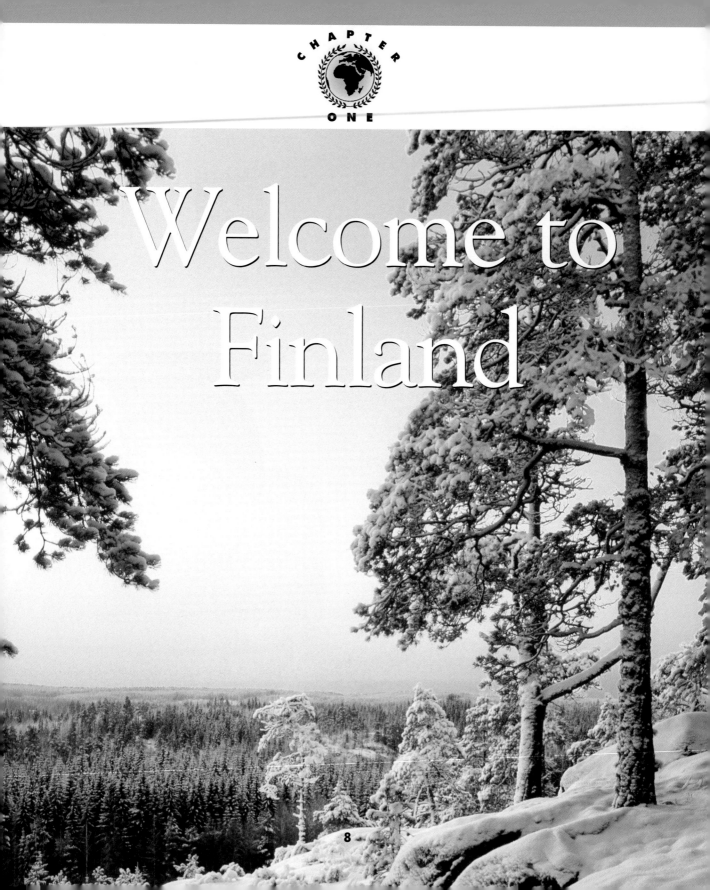

CHAPTER ONE

Welcome to Finland

FINLAND IS AN UNUSUAL COUNTRY IN AN UNUSUAL PLACE. Sitting quietly up at the top of the world, it is surrounded by ice and water, a setting like few others on earth. The natural setting of Finland is appropriate for the Finnish people, who pride themselves on being strong.

The Finns define themselves with the word *sisu*. It's a small word with a lot of meaning. It means courage, stubbornness, endurance, strength, determination, and pride. Finns use this

Opposite: **Finland experiences long, cold winters. About one-third of its land is north of the Arctic Circle.**

A child rides a miniature horse in the countryside.

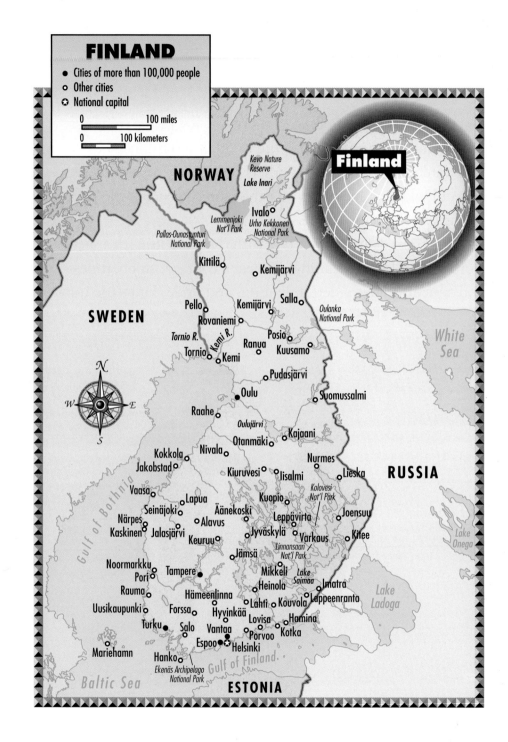

FINLAND

- ● Cities of more than 100,000 people
- ○ Other cities
- ✪ National capital

0   100 miles

0   100 kilometers

Finland

NORWAY

Kevo Nature Reserve

Lake Inari

Lemmenjoki Nat'l Park

Ivalo

Urho Kekkonen National Park

Pallas-Ounastunturi National Park

Kittilä

Kemijärvi

SWEDEN

Pello

Kemijärvi

Salla

Rovaniemi

Oulanka National Park

Tornio R.

Kemi R.

Posio

Tornio

Ranua

Kuusamo

Kemi

Pudasjärvi

White Sea

Oulu

Suomussalmi

Raahe

Oulujärvi

Kajaani

Kokkola

Nivala

Otanmäki

Nurmes

Jakobstad

Kiuruvesi

Iisalmi

Lieska

RUSSIA

Vaasa

Lapua

Kuopio

Kolovesi Nat'l Park

Seinäjoki

Äänekoski

Leppävirta

Joensuu

Närpes

Alavus

Kaskinen

Jalasjärvi

Keuruu

Jyväskylä

Varkaus

Kitee

Jämsä

Linnansaari Nat'l Park

Lake Onega

Noormarkku

Tampere

Mikkeli

Pori

Heinola

Lake Saimaa

Imatra

Rauma

Hämeenlinna

Lahti

Kouvola

Lappeenranta

Lake Ladoga

Uusikaupunki

Forssa

Hyvinkää

Lovisa

Hamina

Turku

Salo

Vantaa

Porvoo

Kotka

Mariehamn

Espoo

✪ Helsinki

Hanko

Ekenäs Archipelago National Park

Gulf of Finland

Baltic Sea

ESTONIA

Gulf of Bothnia

word to talk about their character and their ability to face and conquer challenges.

The challenges the Finnish people have faced have been considerable. They've fought in terrible wars. They've found themselves in the middle of tense international conflicts. They've weathered economic depression and rapidly changing industries. But because of sisu, they've come through it all. Sisu gave the Finns the courage to survive the devastation of World War II, and sisu inspires Finnish athletes to play harder and go faster. Sisu gives new businesses in Finland the daring to jump onto the world stage and make a big impact.

Skiers follow along during a reindeer race in Inari. Reindeer racing is a popular spectator sport in Finland.

Community is important in Finland. People try to help those who need it.

Another word that is important in Finland is *talkoot*. It means "community work." Such work is traditional in Finland. Talkoot could be informal, like helping a friend move to a new apartment, or it could involve an organization such as a church group painting the walls of a local school. In a larger sense, talkoot means cooperation and responsibility. This spirit of cooperation is evident in Finland's generous social programs and opportunities for all. Finns take their freedom and democracy seriously. They work hard to make things right for their people and their environment.

Although the qualities of sisu and talkoot are serious, Finns are also a fun-loving people. Many Finns love the outdoors. They ski and run and bike. They make beautiful ceramics and textiles. They have joyous celebrations. They work hard and they play hard.

Sisu and talkoot, strength and cooperation. These are the backbone of Finland.

Finns celebrate the Midsummer holiday with traditional folk dances.

Land of the Midnight Sun

Winter is the longest season in Finland. The entire country is covered in snow from December to April.

W HEN YOU HEAR THE WORD FINLAND, WHAT COMES TO mind? Snow? Ice? Reindeer? All of those things are accurate. Finland is a snowy, wintry country. It is one of the most northerly countries in the world, with one-third of its area lying above the Arctic Circle. This location makes Finland unusual. But Finland is more than ice and reindeer. It's also a country of wildflowers, berries ripe for picking, rugged coastlines perfect for fishing, thousands of lakes and islands, and the northern lights.

Opposite: **During the summer months in northern Finland, the sun never fully sets. It is visible even in the middle of the night.**

Finland's Geographic Features

Area: 130,559 square miles (338,145 sq km)

Greatest Distance North to South: 717 miles (1,154 km)

Greatest Distance East to West: 336 miles (541 km)

Highest Elevation: Mount Haltia, 4,356 feet (1,328 m)

Lowest Elevation: Sea level, along the coast

Longest River: Kemi River, 340 miles (547 km) long

Largest Lake: Lake Saimaa, 680 square miles (1,761 sq km)

Average High Temperatures: In Helsinki, 72°F (22°C) in July; 27°F (–3°C) in January

Average Low Temperatures: In Helsinki, 55°F (13°C) in July; 16°F (–9°C) in January

Average Annual Precipitation: 27 inches (69 cm)

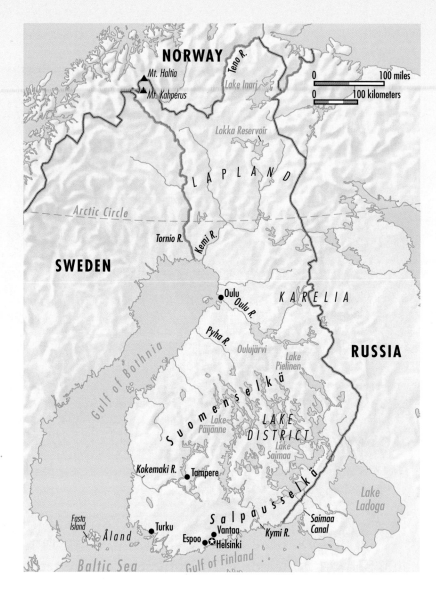

Finding Finland

Finland is part of Scandinavia, a region of northern Europe that also includes Denmark, Sweden, and Norway. Finland shares borders with Norway to the north, Sweden to the northwest, and Russia to the east. The Baltic Sea lies to the south and southwest. The arm of the Baltic along Finland's west coast is called the Gulf of Bothnia, while the part of the Baltic to Finland's south is called the Gulf of Finland.

Finland has about 775 miles (1,250 kilometers) of coastline and more than eighty thousand small islands in the Baltic Sea. The Finnish coastline constantly changes as more land rises up from the sea. Finland is one of the few countries in the world that is growing. It is estimated that Finland gains about 2 square miles (5 sq km) a year. At its greatest extent, Finland

Helsinki sits by the Gulf of Finland. Several islands lie offshore.

Saving a Sea

The Baltic Sea wraps around much of Finland. The Finnish people and economy depend on it. Eight other industrialized nations also line the Baltic. For years, these countries have dumped their waste into it, and the Baltic is now the most polluted sea in the world. It also suffers from serving as one of the world's busiest shipping routes. Collisions produce many small oil spills every year. Now, in some places, the sea is dead. The water contains no oxygen, and no living things of any kind survive there.

To save the sea, the countries that bordered it—Denmark, Finland, Poland, Sweden, and the Soviet Union, East Germany, and West Germany—banded together in 1974 to sign the Helsinki Convention. This agreement tries to protect the Baltic. The flow of dangerous chemicals, such as mercury, into the sea has been cut significantly. Cruise-ship lines have agreed to stop dumping wastewater in the Baltic. Some species in the Baltic are starting to recover. The nations that border the Baltic hope to completely restore the sea's environment by 2021.

measures 717 miles (1,154 km) from north to south and 336 miles (541 km) from east to west. This makes it a little bit smaller than the state of Montana.

Beneath the Ground

Finland lies atop granite, a type of volcanic rock. The granite beneath Finland is about 1.5 billion years old. Glaciers have scraped away at the land over millions of years, leaving the rock exposed. In many places, no soil covers the ground. It is simply bare rock. The Finns value rock as an important natural resource. At many quarries, they cut granite or limestone from the ground. They also remove minerals—mostly copper and zinc—from the rock.

This granite hill in Roismala is now a giant hole after all the granite was quarried out.

In winter months in northern Finland, the sun does not rise above the horizon for days.

Midnight Sun and Polar Night

Finland is one of a small group of nations that have territory above the Arctic Circle. Finland's northerly location gives it an unusual feature—the midnight sun.

The farther north or south a place is on the globe, the more dramatically the length of days varies throughout the year. The earth is tilted on its axis as it circles the sun. In the summer, that tilt points the North Pole toward the sun twenty-four hours a day.

The sun never sets in parts of Finland during the summer. The northernmost parts of the country have about seventy days of continuous sun. In the capital, Helsinki, which lies in the southern part of the country, the sun goes down for only about five hours a day during the summer.

During the winter, everything is reversed. The North Pole points away from the sun throughout the day, and the sun never rises in some parts of Finland. This is called the polar night. Finns in the northern reaches of the country live without the sun for about fifty days a year. On the shortest day of the year—December 21—the sun shines for only six hours in Helsinki.

The Northern Lights

One of the splendors of Finland occurs during the long winter nights. The sky lights up with brilliant bursts of colored light. This is the aurora borealis, or northern lights. It is caused by charged particles from the sun hitting the earth's atmosphere. It is most often seen in northerly parts of the world. In northern Finland, the aurora borealis appears as many as two hundred times a year. In southern Finland, it may be visible only fifteen times a year. The same phenomenon, called the southern lights, occurs near the South Pole.

Ancient people who witnessed the aurora explained it in different ways. In Finnish, the auroras are called *revontulet*, which means "fox fires." The Finns have a folktale about an arctic fox starting fires with its tail. It shot sparks into the sky, forming the auroras. The Sámi people, who live in the northern part of Finland known as Lapland, believed that people should remain silent when witnessing the lights. Praise or criticism could anger the lights, inciting them to kill their viewers.

The Coastal Lowlands

Finland is divided into several regions, each with its own character and climate. Most Finns live in the coastal lowlands, which are between 40 and 80 miles (65 and 130 km) wide and hug the coast along the Baltic Sea from Sweden to Russia. The major cities of Helsinki, Espoo, and Turku are in this region. In some ways, this is the easiest place to live in Finland. The coastal lowlands are flat, with few forests and easy access to the sea. Rivers flow through the coastal lowlands to the Baltic Sea, making it easy for boats to travel through the region.

The land in the coastal lowlands is flatter than in the rest of the country. Most Finns live in this region.

Finland's best agricultural land is in the coastal lowlands, and most of Finland's seventy thousand farms are found there. Farmers in Finland grow mainly grains, such as barley, oats, wheat, potatoes, and rye.

The Coastal Islands

Finland has more than 180,000 small islands, mostly scattered in the Baltic. Some, called skerries, are too small even to build a house on. About twenty-five thousand people live on the Åland Islands, which lie in the Baltic Sea between Sweden and Finland, off the coast of Turku. Although the Åland Islands technically belong to Finland, they are a self-governing region with their own parliament. The islands have a mild climate that supports a long growing season.

Bridges connect many of the Åland Islands. Nearly half of the people on the islands live in the town of Mariehamn.

Houseboats line the shore-
line of Lake Saimaa in the
summer months.

The Lake District

Finland is a land of lakes. The nation has about 190,000 lakes of all sizes. The lakes formed about ten thousand years ago, during the last ice age. Slow-moving glaciers gouged lake beds out of the granite. As the earth warmed and the land rose, the glaciers melted, their water filling the beds to create lakes.

Most of Finland's lakes are in the Lake District, which spreads across the southeast of the country. The district is physically separated from the coastal lowlands by the Salpausselkä ridges.

About fourteen thousand islands dot Lake Saimaa. These islands formed at the end of the last ice age from the gravel left behind by melting glaciers.

About one-fourth of the area in the Lake District is water. The rest is forest. The largest lake in Finland is Lake Saimaa, which covers more than 680 square miles (1,761 sq km). The lake is linked to Vyborg, Russia, by the 35-mile (56 km) Saimaa Canal, which opened in 1856. The canal is a major transportation route through the area. A number of smaller canals and smaller lakes link to form one large waterway. Lake Päijänne, the second-largest lake in Finland, drains south into the Gulf of Finland by way of the Kymi River.

The Lake District is important in the lives of Finns, even those who don't live there. Many Finns own or rent vacation homes in the district, and families flock there in summertime. In winter, the shallow lakes and waterways freeze and can host winter fun like skating, sledding, skiing, and ice fishing.

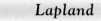
The northernmost part of Finland, called Lapland, lies within the Arctic Circle. This region is mostly high plateaus, lakes, and swampland. Finland's highest mountain is in Lapland. Mount Haltia, which reaches 4,356 feet (1,328 meters), is part of a small ridge of mountains that borders Sweden and Norway.

Lapland is where reindeer come from. It is also the traditional home of the Sámi people. For thousands of years, they lived in the far north, herding reindeer and hunting. A few Sámi continue to live this way.

A Sámi reindeer farmer leads his herd through the snow. Lapland is the traditional home of the Sámi people.

Lapland is Finland's Land of the Midnight Sun. It attracts summertime visitors, who come to linger in the endless days.

Although Finland is far north and dark for much of the year, it is not as cold as some other northerly regions. Much of this is due to the Gulf Stream, a powerful ocean current that carries warm waters from the Gulf of Mexico north to the Baltic Sea.

Southern Finland (where most Finns live) has a northern temperate climate, the same as the northern United States and southern Canada. Winters are long and cold, with temperatures rarely rising above freezing. In Lapland, temperatures sometimes drop as low as –58 degrees Fahrenheit (–50 degrees Celsius).

Winter begins early in the far north of the country—around mid-October—and slowly creeps south until it reaches the southernmost islands in December. Most people in Finland consider November the start of winter. That is when snow begins to fall. It quickly covers the ground and does not melt until April or May. Winter lasts about one hundred days in the southernmost part of Finland and about two hundred days in Lapland.

Helsinki residents enjoy the sun at a city park. Finns try to make the most of the short summer season.

Looking at Finland's Cities

Helsinki is Finland's capital and largest city, with 564,521 residents. Espoo, Finland's second-largest city (population 235,019), and Vantaa, Finland's fourth-largest city (population 189,711), lie on the southern coast. They are both near Helsinki and are considered part of the Helsinki metropolitan area. The population of Espoo has increased tenfold since the mid-twentieth century, and Espoo is now home to many science and technology companies.

Tampere (right), Finland's third-largest city, with a population of 206,638, is the nation's major inland city. Tampere began as a market town during the 1700s. By the mid-1800s, it had grown into an industrial powerhouse. The city's factories produced huge quantities of metal and textiles. Most of these factories

are now gone. Today, the people of Tampere work in telecommunications and other technology industries.

Turku, the nation's fifth-largest city with 175,354 residents, lies on the southwestern coast. It is the oldest city in Finland, and it was once the capital. Although people have lived in the region of Turku for thousands of years, the city itself was not founded until the 1200s. Soon, a castle and a cathedral were built, and the city became the center of medieval Finland. Today, it is a major port city, an education center, and the home of thriving high-tech industries. The city also boasts many notable museums, including the Turku Art Museum and the Turku Castle and Historical Museum (left).

The ice sheet on a river slowly melts away—a sure sign that spring is coming.

Spring is a short season in Finland, lasting only about fifty days. It comes to the south of Finland in April and slowly edges north, reaching Lapland in early May. It takes about a month for the snow and ice to melt. Once that happens and the temperature rises above 40°F (5°C), plants can begin to grow. The lakes in Finland's interior are usually melted in May and June.

Summers are pleasant in Finland. Summer begins in late May in the south and has reached all parts of the country by late June. The season lasts until mid-September. The average high in Helsinki in July is a pleasant 72°F (22°C), but in the middle of the country, away from the sea, it can get hot.

Sometimes the temperature soars to 95°F (35°C). Many summer afternoons see short bursts of rain. This rain combines with long days and warm sun to give plants a chance to thrive during their short growing season.

Like winter, autumn starts in the north and moves southward. Autumn begins around the last week of August in northern Finland and takes a month to reach the southern islands. And then, once again, it is time to return to the cold, dark winter.

Colorful autumn leaves light up the hills in Urho Kekkonen National Park. The sign marks a trail that will soon be ready for snowmobiles.

Wild Things

FINLAND IS A LAND OF WATER AND TREES. TREES COVER MORE than two-thirds of the country, and lakes and rivers cover about one-tenth of the country. The Baltic Sea makes up almost half of Finland's border. Nature is important economically, historically, and culturally to Finland. To talk about Finland is to talk about its environment.

Opposite: **A great gray owl perches in a tree. These huge birds hunt mice in the frozen fields of the north.**

Pine trees can withstand long winters and are common throughout Finland.

Much of Finland is coniferous, or cone-bearing, forest. Spruce trees are most common in the south of the country, and pine trees are more common in the north. The southern part of the country also has a zone of deciduous trees (trees that lose their leaves in winter) including birch, hazel, aspen, maple,

Birch trees grow as far north as Urho Kekkonen National Park in Lapland. They are easily identified by their white trunks.

Everyman's Right

Everyman's Right is an ancient tradition in Finland that has become law. Everyman's Right allows all Finns to use the land and waterways free of charge and without having to ask permission, even if the land is private property. Those who use the land agree to do so respectfully.

Everyone may:
- walk, ski, or cycle in the countryside, except in gardens, in people's yards, and in fields that could be damaged
- set up camp in the countryside
- pick wild berries, mushrooms, and flowers if they are not protected species
- fish with a rod and line
- row, sail, or use a motorboat on waterways
- swim in inland waters and the sea
- walk, ski, and fish on frozen waterways

What is not allowed:
- disturbing other people or damaging property
- disturbing breeding birds, their nests, and their chicks
- disturbing reindeer or game animals
- cutting down or damaging living trees or collecting wood, moss, or lichen on private property
- lighting open fires on private property
- littering
- driving a car off-road on private property
- fishing or hunting without a permit

elm, linden, and alder. In many places, there is little or no soil on the rocky ground, but the trees have adapted to be able to survive under these conditions. Trees are Finland's most valuable natural resource, and the country is a leading producer of wood and wood products.

More than twelve hundred species of plants survive in Finland's cold climate and rocky terrain. Finland is also home to eight hundred different mosses and more than one thousand kinds of lichens. All of these have adapted to live in Finland's cold climate. Some go dormant in the winter and grow rapidly during the warmer seasons.

Many native plants of Finland are edible. Lingonberries, cowberries, blueberries, and thimbleberries are everywhere

Lingonberries are an important part of Finnish cuisine. They are picked from July to October.

in the summer. So are many kinds of mushrooms. In Finland, a law known as Everyman's Right permits everyone to pick these wild foods on both public and private land. As a result, many Finns gather mushrooms and berries.

Animals

For a relatively small country, Finland has many wild animals. At least 60 species of mammals, along with 450 kinds of birds, 70 kinds of fish, and a handful of reptiles and amphibians make a home in Finland.

Some mammals in Finland are large and dramatic. Finland is home to all four of Europe's large predators: the brown bear, the wolf, the wolverine, and the lynx. These animals have been hunted for several hundred years, but strong conservation efforts are keeping their numbers stable and allowing them to thrive.

A European brown bear leads her cubs in a northern forest. This species lives mostly in northern Europe and Russia.

Other large mammals in Finland include reindeer and elk. Elk are so plentiful that there are about two thousand car accidents a year involving them. Reindeer are not actually wild animals. Reindeer are a domesticated species kept for thousands of years by the Sámi herders of Lapland, who allow them to roam freely. Finland's forests also shelter smaller mammals like red foxes and mountain hares, and in its waters live otters and seals.

Red foxes belong to the same family as wolves and domestic dogs. They prey on smaller mammals such as mice.

The Saimaa Ringed Seal

The Saimaa ringed seal is one of the most endangered seals in the world. Only about 270 of them remain, and the only place they live is in Lake Saimaa. These seals make their lairs, or homes, in snowdrifts on the ice on the surface of Lake Saimaa. The mother seal has one pup in February. She makes a hole in the floor of her ice den, slips into the water to look for food, and then returns to care for her pup. Once spring comes, the pups head out to learn to swim with their mothers.

The biggest threat to the Saimaa ringed seal is fishing nets. Between 50 and 60 seal pups are born in Lake Saimaa each year. But scientists estimate that 10 to 20 of them get caught in fishing nets and die. They believe that if all these pups survived, the seal population could recover. The government restricts fishing and land use near the seals' main breeding grounds, but some seals breed outside of the protected areas. The pups born there are at risk.

Another danger is fluctuating water levels. If the level of the water in Lake Saimaa rises too much, it can flood the seals' lairs. If the water level drops too low, the ice on the bottom of the lairs can crack, which destroys the lairs. The Finnish government tries to keep the water level in the lake stable to help protect the seals.

The Siberian flying squirrel is the only flying squirrel species in Europe. They nest in hollow trees throughout Scandinavia and Russia.

Like its plants, Finland's animals have adapted to the rough winters. Some, like hares and foxes, grow thick fur in winter. Squirrels and arctic foxes change their coloring. The arctic fox grows a white coat, which causes it to blend in with the snow, making it a better hunter. The squirrel turns the same gray as the branches of the trees it lives in, helping it hide from predators. Other animals and many birds dig burrows in the snow to stay warm.

Finland's forests and coasts attract a large variety of birds. Hazel hens, grouse, white-tailed eagles, and ptarmigans live in the forest. As many as ten species of owls live in the country, including the pygmy owl and the Tengmalm's owl. Finland is also home to many large waterbirds, such as the whooper swan and the crane. Huge numbers of arctic birds, including eider ducks and guillemots, fly over Finland during their spring and fall migrations. Thousands of acres of Finnish land have been set aside as nature preserves for these migrating birds. Humans are not allowed in most of these areas during the busiest migration times.

Hazel grouse feed on berries, worms, and insects. They live in northern Europe and northern Asia.

Winter Sleep

In Finland, many animals, including bears, hedgehogs (right), badgers, and bats, hibernate in the winter. That is, they spend much of the winter sleeping in caves, dens, or other safe places. Over the winter, their bodies slow down and they need little food. By staying dormant, in a sleeplike state, they conserve their energy. Being in a den also protects them from predators. Once the ice thaws and berries, leaves, and other foods begin to reappear, the animals wake up and head back out into the world.

Environmental Protection

Finland's economy has long relied on its natural resources. Finns cut down trees to make houses, furniture, and paper. Yet many tourists visit Finland to see its glorious landscape. This

National Nature Symbols

In the 1980s and 1990s, Finland held a series of national votes in which citizens chose national nature symbols. The government hoped that this program would encourage Finns to pay attention to and protect these natural treasures. The six national nature symbols of Finland are:

Bear: In Finland, the bear is called the king of the forest and is important in folk stories and songs. Bears are feared and respected in Finland, and today bear hunts are limited.

Swan: The whooper swan was sacred to many of the ancient people of Finland. The bird became severely endangered in the twentieth century, but its numbers rebounded after Finland began programs to protect it.

Perch: Finland's most common fish is the perch. Fishers reel in millions of perch every year.

Birch: In Finland, birch has been used to make everything from fires to baskets. Finns also make a drink from birch sap.

Lily-of-the-Valley: This wildflower grows all over Finland and has a strong scent.

Granite: Finland's granite is ancient, dating from about 1.5 billion years ago. The landscape of Finland is unusual because it has lots of exposed granite.

National Parks

Finland boasts thirty-five national parks. Lemmenjoki is the country's largest national park. Located in Lapland, it's a great place for hiking, boating, and even panning for gold. Urho Kekkonen National Park (above) is also in Lapland and features reindeer and old Sámi settlements for visitors to see. Ekenäs Archipelago is on the southern coast of Finland and showcases the islands' seals and seabirds.

is one reason why the people of Finland work to protect their environment.

Finland's environmental policy is based on the idea that it is easier to prevent a problem then to fix a problem once it happens. So the country has tried hard to protect and manage its environment. For example, Finland's forests are used for industry, but they are also managed. After mature trees are cut down, new trees are planted to replace them. These policies seem to be working. Finland has been rated among the world's leading countries in terms of protecting the environment.

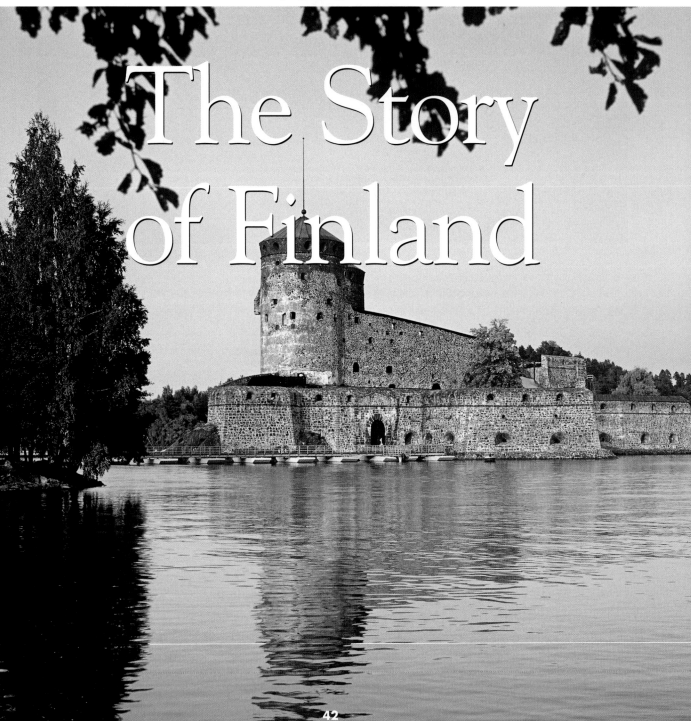

The Story of Finland

THE LAST SEVERAL THOUSAND YEARS HAVE SEEN A LOT OF change in Finland. People first settled there in about 8500 B.C. For a long time, several tribes of people who hunted and fished inhabited Finland, including Finns, Tavastians, and Karelians. Some evidence suggests that these people both fought and traded with each other. They also had contact with people from what are now Estonia and Sweden.

A man dressed as a stone-age resident of Finland walks toward a hut at the Kierikki Stone Age Center. Visitors to the center learn about Finland's prehistoric culture.

Opposite: The Olavinlinna Castle was built in the 1400s. Over the centuries, both Sweden and Russia controlled the castle.

Two Castles

Finland has a number of medieval castles that have survived the ages. Two of the most significant are Turku Castle (below) and Häme Castle (right).

Around 1280, Turku was a thriving trade center and the base of Finland's government. At that time, the governor of Finland had Turku Castle built as a fortress, complete with a square fort and two towers. The governor himself lived behind its strong stone walls. Over hundreds of years, the castle grew to include more

than forty rooms, with a banquet hall, a shooting gallery, and quarters for the king and queen when they visited from Sweden. Turku Castle withstood six sieges and many battles over the years. It fell into ruin until it was restored and opened as a museum in the twentieth century. Today, more people visit Turku Castle than any museum in Finland.

Häme Castle also dates from the late thirteenth century. Most of the castle is built out of brick, which was unusual for a castle built in the Middle Ages, when carved stone was the usual building material. Häme Castle has had many different purposes during its long history, serving as everything from fortress to storehouse to prison. Today, it is a historical monument.

By the eleventh century, Finland's neighbors—Sweden, to Finland's west, and the Republic of Novgorod (part of today's Russia), to the east—had taken notice of it. At the time, Sweden was Roman Catholic and Novgorod was Orthodox. Beginning in about 1050, the two countries sent missionaries to Finland to spread their religions. These two groups clashed in Finland and battled over the land. In 1323, a peace treaty divided Finland. Sweden took the west and the south, while the eastern Karelian region belonged to Novgorod.

The Time of Swedish Rule

For about six hundred years, the Swedes' way of life took over in Finland, which they called Osterland, meaning "Land to the East." The Finns lived under Swedish legal and social rule, and in many ways, they were treated well. They were allowed to vote and to have representatives in government, both in Finland and, eventually, in Sweden.

In 1397, Sweden (and therefore Finland) became part of the Kingdom of Denmark. In 1523, the Swedish king Gustavus Vasa cut Sweden-Finland's ties to Denmark. Swedish became the official language of the land. During much of the time it ruled

Divided Finland, 1323

Republic of Novgorod   Sweden

Present-day Finland

Finland, Sweden was a great power in Europe. But Sweden was also often at war with its neighbors, including Denmark, Poland, and Russia. Many Finns fought in these wars.

During this time, the Catholic Church was powerful throughout Europe. But in the 1500s, some people, including Martin Luther in Germany, began challenging the Catholic Church's authority. They questioned some of the church's ideas and practices. Their reform movement, called the Reformation, split from the Catholic Church, creating a new branch of Christianity, Protestantism. A clergyman named Mikael Agricola helped bring the Protestant Reformation to Finland. Agricola translated the New Testament into Finnish and set off a wave of interest in the Finnish language and Finnish folklore. In 1554, he became the first Lutheran bishop in Finland.

In the 1700s, Sweden began to decline as a European power. From 1700 to 1721, Sweden lost the Great Northern War against Russia, Poland, and Denmark. The war ended with Sweden giving Russia land in southern and eastern Finland.

In 1709, the Battle of Poltava was fought in what is now Ukraine. It was an important victory for Russia in the Great Northern War.

Alexander I ruled Russia from 1801 to 1825. His army invaded Finland in 1808.

The Time of Russian Rule

By 1800, skirmishes over parts of Finland were becoming common. Sweden was weakening, and other nations looked for ways to conquer parts of the Swedish Empire. In 1808, Russia, under Emperor Alexander I, invaded Finland. A short war followed, and in 1809, Russia took Finland from Sweden. Finland was now called the Russian Grand Duchy of Finland. Although it was part of the Russian Empire, its laws and government differed from those in the rest of the empire. Nothing much changed for the people of Finland, except that Alexander moved the capital of Finland from Turku to Helsinki, which was closer to the Russian capital of St. Petersburg.

The main building of the University of Helsinki was completed in 1832. It stands by Senate Square across from the building that housed the national senate at the time.

For the most part, the Russian era was a time of peace and advancement in Finland. Alexander I rebuilt Helsinki, which had been damaged by war and fires. Finland's university followed the capital by moving from Turku to Helsinki in 1828. The Saimaa Canal opened in 1856, providing a way for people to move goods through the watery interior of Finland.

"Let Us Be Finns"

The Russian era also saw a rise in Finnish nationalism. For seven hundred years, the Finnish people had been ruled by other nations—first Sweden and then Russia. In the nineteenth century, more and more Finns simply wanted to be Finnish. A popular slogan at the time was "Swedes we are no longer, Russians we can never become, so let us be Finns!" Scholars and writers took pride in the Finnish language and started producing works in Finnish. The *Kalevala*, the Finnish national epic poem, was published in 1835. In 1863, Emperor Alexander II of Russia issued a decree that started the process of making Finnish the official language of the land.

Finland faced tough times right after independence. A flu epidemic swept the globe in 1918 and 1919, killing millions of people. Twenty-five thousand Finns died from the flu, and the new nation faced shortages of food and medical equipment.

But life soon began improving in the new nation. The lumber industry took off, and agricultural production grew. Finland's economy expanded, and the country built an international reputation for always repaying its debts.

Finland also started strong social welfare policies during this time. Finns believe nations are responsible for taking care of all of their citizens. Finland established programs that provided care and services for children, the poor, and the elderly.

Life was difficult in Finland immediately after independence. Here, children line up for a free meal.

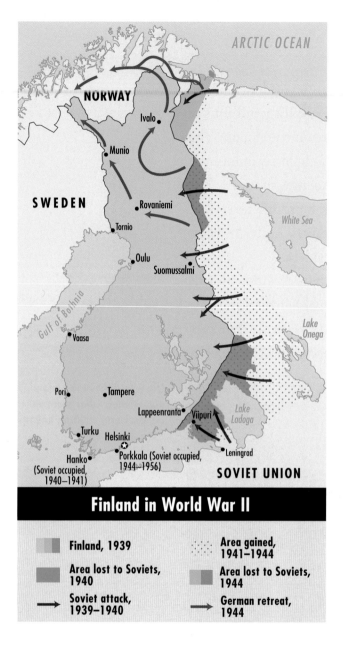

Finland in World War II

▨ Finland, 1939	⠿ Area gained, 1941–1944
▨ Area lost to Soviets, 1940	▨ Area lost to Soviets, 1944
→ Soviet attack, 1939–1940	→ German retreat, 1944

Map labels: ARCTIC OCEAN; NORWAY; Ivalo; Munio; SWEDEN; Rovaniemi; Tornio; White Sea; Oulu; Suomussalmi; Gulf of Bothnia; Vaasa; Lake Onega; Pori; Tampere; Lake Ladoga; Lappeenranta; Viipuri; Turku; Helsinki; Hanko (Soviet occupied, 1940–1941); Porkkala (Soviet occupied, 1944–1956); Leningrad; SOVIET UNION

World War II

Germany became aggressive toward its neighbors during the 1930s, after the Nazi Party came to power. In 1939, Germany invaded Poland. Great Britain and France then declared war on Germany. World War II had begun.

Finland at first declared itself neutral in the war. By this time, Russia had combined with several neighboring states to create a huge country called the Soviet Union. The Soviet Union wanted to secure the safety of Leningrad (today's St. Petersburg), its second-largest city, which lay near Finland. To protect Leningrad, the Soviet Union demanded that Finland give up some territory. When Finland refused, the Soviets invaded, and so began what became known as the Winter War.

The war started in November 1939 and lasted four months. The Soviet army overpowered the Finnish army, and no other nation came forward to help Finland. Seventy thousand Finns were killed or wounded in the short war. In negotiations for peace, Finland was forced to give up a large piece of Karelia, a region in the east, including the city of Viipuri. The country also lost islands in the Gulf of Finland, a naval base, and land in northeastern Finland. The people who lived in these areas moved to Finnish-controlled lands to escape Soviet rule.

In 1940, the Finns turned to Germany for help protecting themselves from the Soviets. The Germans attacked the Soviets on June 22, 1941, and in retaliation, the Soviets attacked Finland. On June 25, Finland declared war on the Soviet Union. This second war between the Soviet Union and Finland is called the Continuation War.

German and Finnish soldiers stationed in northern Finland during the Winter War

The Continuation War was worse than the Winter War. One in ten Finnish soldiers died or was wounded. The war dragged on until it became certain that the Soviet Union would defeat Germany. In 1944, Finland asked for peace talks. As a condition for peace, the Soviets demanded that Finland throw German troops out of Finland. Finland was

Finnish soldiers approach German troops in October 1944, during the Lapland War.

now forced to fight its former ally in the Lapland War of 1944–1945. Finnish Lapland, about one-third of the country, was burned to the ground by German troops as they withdrew into Norway in the face of Finnish attacks.

Postwar Rebuilding

Finns faced a difficult task in rebuilding their country after World War II. The Soviets demanded that Finland send them goods worth about US$300 million as war reparations to help pay for the cost of the war. The Finns took paying their debts seriously. They set about strengthening their industries so that they had the means to repay the Soviet Union. In the long run, Finland's debt burden proved helpful, because it prompted the country to build a strong industrial and export economy, both of which would serve it well for years to come. Paying off the debts also helped repair Finland's relationship with the Soviet Union. Long after the reparations had been paid, the two countries remained trading partners, to the benefit of both.

After the war, Finland helped resettle thousands of refugees who had fled Soviet-controlled areas. The Land Act of 1945 required that the government purchase land and give it to refugees and Finnish soldiers who had fought in the war.

Living Through the Cold War

The Soviet Union and the United States had been allies in the effort to defeat Germany in World War II. But after the war, they became bitter enemies. The Soviet Union was communist, and many Americans were afraid that the Soviets would try to spread communism to other parts of the world. Neither country trusted the other, and both began building up their militaries for fear that the other would attack. This period of tense competition and conflict between the United States and the Soviet Union is called the cold war.

The Berlin War separated Soviet-controlled East Germany from West Germany during the cold war.

Finland hoped to remain neutral in the cold war. The Finns wanted to stay on friendly terms with their powerful neighbor yet still maintain their freedom. On April 6, 1948, Finland and the Soviet Union signed the Treaty of Friendship, Cooperation, and Mutual Assistance. Some European nations criticized Finland for being too friendly with the Soviets. But Finland used this treaty and its trade relations with the Soviets to remain free and separate from the Soviet Union, even while nearby nations in Eastern Europe were falling under Soviet influence and control.

Soviet troops in Bulgaria. Finland managed to avoid Soviet domination after World War II, unlike Bulgaria and most of Eastern Europe.

The European Union accepted ten new nations in 2004, including Finland. Finnish prime minister Matti Vanhanen (far left) stood with leaders of the other new EU countries at a ceremony marking the occasion.

Finland managed to walk this line between East and West for decades. Meanwhile, the Finnish economy was booming. In the years after the war, Finland changed from an agricultural country to a modern, industrialized nation.

Then, in 1991, the Soviet Union collapsed, breaking apart into many different nations. Finland's economy suffered because the Soviet Union had been one of its major trade partners. The Finnish unemployment rate shot up to 17 percent.

By the mid-1990s, however, the economy had stabilized. Finland was increasingly oriented toward Western Europe. In 1995, Finland joined the European Union (EU), an economic and political group that today includes twenty-seven European nations. The EU member states share an economic policy, which has helped strengthen the economies of many member states. Today, Finland enjoys good relations with all of its neighbors.

Government
by the People

60

IN 2017, FINLAND WILL CELEBRATE ITS FIRST CENTURY AS an independent republic. Finns take pride in their democracy and take their responsibilities as citizens of a republic seriously. They take their political opinions seriously too—Finland sometimes has dozens of political parties. Finns can vote starting at age eighteen, and about 70 percent of Finns show up to vote in all elections.

The powers of the Finnish government are divided among three branches. They are the executive, legislative, and judicial.

Opposite: **A son helps his mother drop her ballot in the box during the 2006 presidential election.**

Finnish president Tarja Halonen (right) speaks at the opening session of the Finnish parliament in 2007. She took the opportunity to encourage more Finns to vote in future elections.

Urho Kaleva Kekkonen

Urho Kaleva Kekkonen served as president of Finland for twenty-six years beginning in 1956. Kekkonen was born in 1900 and had a distinguished political career

before he was elected president, serving as minister of justice, minister of the interior, and prime minister.

As president, Kekkonen was a controversial figure. A great deal of internal conflict flared in the Finnish government while he held office. On several occasions, he dissolved parliament and called for new elections to steer decisions on national issues his way. Still, he continued to get reelected and was able to convince members of differing groups to agree on many issues.

Part of Kekkonen's popularity had to do with his ability to manage Finland's relations with the Soviet Union. During the cold war, Finland found itself in a delicate position: it was a small democracy next to the communist superpower. Kekkonen adopted a policy of "active neutrality," in which Finland supported policies that allowed the nations of the world to avoid violence. This policy helped Finland maintain friendly relations with the United States and its allies as well as with the Soviet Union and its allies. Urho Kekkonen retired from office in 1982 and died in 1986.

The Executive Branch

The executive branch of the government consists of the president and the Council of State, or Valtioneuvosto (Statsrådet in Swedish). The president must be a native-born Finn. The people elect him or her to a six-year term of office. The longest-serving president was Urho Kaleva Kekkonen, who was elected four times. Since 1991, presidents have been allowed to serve only two terms. The president is the head of state. He or she is the commander in chief of the armed forces and is involved in the nation's foreign policy. In 2000, Tarja Halonen was elected president, becoming the first woman to hold the office. She was reelected in 2006.

The prime minister is the head of the government. He or she is chosen by parliament and then officially appointed by the president. The prime minister nominates other cabinet members such as minister of defense and minister of education. Together, they form the Council of State.

Matti Vanhanen became prime minister of Finland in 2003.

NATIONAL GOVERNMENT OF FINLAND

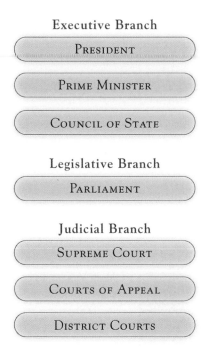

Executive Branch

PRESIDENT

PRIME MINISTER

COUNCIL OF STATE

Legislative Branch

PARLIAMENT

Judicial Branch

SUPREME COURT

COURTS OF APPEAL

DISTRICT COURTS

The Legislative Branch

The legislative branch of government is the parliament, called the Eduskunta (Riksdag in Swedish, Finland's second official language). Its members pass laws, approve the national budget, and supervise the way the country is run.

Finns elect two hundred members of parliament, who serve four-year terms. The members of parliament win their seats based on proportional representation. This means that the percentage of votes that a party gets in an election determines the percentage of seats that party will hold in parliament. Finland has many major political parties, so it's not unusual for more than ten parties to be represented in parliament.

A session of the Finnish parliament meets in 2007. Parliamentary elections are held on the third Sunday in March.

The Judicial Branch

The judicial branch of the government is the court system, which has three levels: district courts, courts of appeal, and the Supreme Court. There is no trial by jury in Finland. Instead, judges render the verdicts in all cases. But district courts often use a panel made up of a professional judge and three "lay judges" who are elected by city councils. Like being a juror in the United States, being a lay judge is a civic duty, not a job. The lay judges generally are involved in only one hearing a month, for which they receive a small fee and payment for lost income.

In 2004, the Finnish Supreme Court made a controversial ruling that ordered a Finnish mother to take her two sons to the United States to be reunited with their father. Many Finns protested the decision.

Female Firsts

In 1906, Finland became the first country in Europe to grant all citizens—female and male—the right to vote. Before that, women had had no voting rights at all. That same year, Finnish women got the right to run for parliamentary office. This made the Eduskunta the first parliament in the world to allow women to hold office. In 1907, during the first elections after this change, Finns elected nineteen women to parliament.

The Flag

The flag of Finland shows an off-center blue cross on a white field. The colors represent the nature of Finland: blue is for Finland's lakes, and white is for the winter snows.

District courts hear criminal cases, civil cases, and matters such as divorce and child custody. The decision of a district court can be appealed in one of six courts of appeal, located in Helsinki, Turku, Vaasa, Kouvola, Kuopio, and Rovaniemi.

Courts of appeal also hear the first trial of higher crimes such as treason. Decisions of the courts of appeal may be appealed in the Supreme Court. The Supreme Court is made up of a president and eighteen justices. In addition to hearing appeals, the Supreme Court rules on matters of law that affect the governing of the entire country.

Provincial and Local Government

Finland is divided into six provinces. Each province is run by a governor who is appointed by the president. The provincial governments are responsible for social services and health care; education and culture, police administration, rescue services, traffic administration, consumer affairs, and judicial administration.

On the local level, each community has a municipal council. Its members are elected for four-year terms. The size of the council is related to the population—the larger the community, the larger the council. Municipalities control many community services, such as schooling, health care, the water supply, and maintaining local streets.

Foreign Policy

Finland is a small country, but it has a long history of involvement in world affairs. This tradition continues today. Finland is a member of several international organizations, including the European Union and the Nordic Council.

Finland spent most of the twentieth century in the middle of the cold war, squeezed between the United States and the Soviet Union. The small nation walked the line well and was the only country in the world that maintained good trade and diplomatic ties to nations on both sides in the cold war. To do this, Finland remained neutral, distinguishing itself from most Western European nations.

When the Soviet Union broke apart in 1991 and the cold war ended, Finland had to redefine itself. Its old strategy would no longer benefit the nation, politically or economically. Finland took up this challenge and succeeded.

The National Anthem

When bands are asked to play the Finnish national anthem, they get out the music for a song called "Maame" in Finnish and "Vårt Land" in Swedish. The song's title means "Our Land." Johan Ludvig Runeberg, a Swedish-speaking poet, wrote the lyrics, and Frederick Pacius wrote the music. The song was first performed in 1848. Although Finns have long considered the song Finland's national anthem, the Finnish government has never officially declared it so.

Our land, our land, our fatherland,
Sound loud, O name of worth!
No mount that meets the heaven's band,
No hidden vale, no wavewashed strand,
Is loved, as is our native North, our own forefathers'
  earth.
Thy blossom, in the bud laid low,
Yet ripened shall upspring.
See! From our love once more shall grow
Thy light, thy joy, thy hope, thy glow!
And clearer yet one day shall ring
The song our land shall sing.

The European Union

Since 1995, Finland has been a member of the European Union (EU), a political and economic community that now includes twenty-seven countries. The members of the EU share a system of laws that govern trade and the movement of people among member nations. The goal of the EU is to promote peace and cooperation in Europe while respecting the special qualities of each member nation. A president heads the EU. The office of EU president changes hands every six months, rotating among the member nations.

As a member of the EU, Finland belongs to the larger European community. The EU has eliminated most trade restrictions among member countries, allowing goods and people to move more freely within Europe.

The European parliament governs the European Union. The parliament meets in Brussels, Belgium.

The Nordic Council

Finland has been a member of the Nordic Council since the mid-1950s. The council is made up of the countries of Finland, Iceland, Norway, and Sweden and the territories of the Faroe Islands, Greenland, and the Åland Islands. In many ways, the Nordic Council was a preview of what the EU has become. The council made agreements that allowed

President Tarja Halonen (far left) escorts Japanese emperor Akihito in an inspection of the Finnish guard of honor on a visit in 2000.

citizens of its member nations to move freely from country to country and made some of the nations' laws more similar.

Finland's Military

The Finnish defense forces consist of an army, navy, and air force. Finland requires that all young men serve in the military for a period of six months to one year, depending on the kind of training they receive. As an alternative, they can choose to serve thirteen months of nonmilitary service. Young men typically serve after finishing their schooling. Young women can volunteer to serve, but it is not required.

The Åland Islands

The Åland Islands hold a unique place in Finnish government. Åland belongs to Finland but governs itself. It has its own parliament, which functions separately from the parliament of Finland. Most island residents speak Swedish. Åland also has a membership in the Nordic Council separate from Finland's.

Helsinki: Did You Know This?

Finland's capital, Helsinki, is the largest city in the country and the center of government, culture, and business. Helsinki was bombed during World War II but did not suffer large-scale destruction. Since then, Helsinki has grown into a thriving modern city.

In 1952, Helsinki gained world attention when it hosted the Summer Olympics. Because of its location between the East and the West of the cold war period, diplomats from other countries have often chosen Helskinki as the site for their international talks.

In 1969, the Soviet Union and the United States went to Helsinki for the Strategic Arms Limitation Talks (SALT), their first meetings to control nuclear weapons. In 1975, talks in Finland's capital produced the Helsinki Accords, an agreement among the United States, Canada, the Soviet Union, and European nations intended to limit cold-war tensions.

The green-domed Lutheran Cathedral is the symbol of Helsinki. The city is also home to the National Museum of Finland, which features artifacts from thousands of years of history. Helsinki's many art museums and galleries include the Ateneum Art Museum, which displays classical art, and the Kiasma Museum, which displays contemporary art.

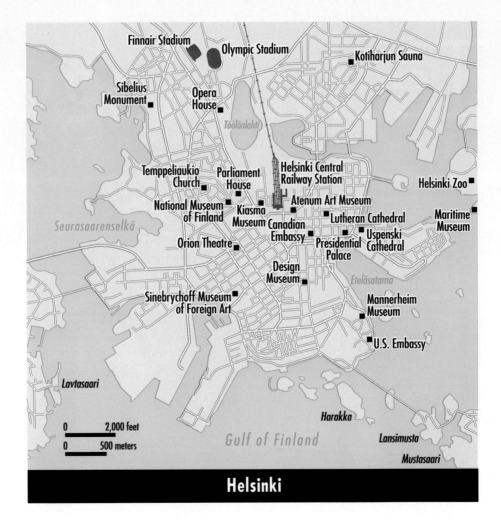

Helsinki

From Trees to Technology

Nokia Corporation is the largest mobile telephone manufacturer in the world. It is headquartered in Espoo, near Helsinki.

I F YOU WANT TO SEE HOW A COUNTRY CAN CHANGE ITS economy and workforce in a short period of time, look at Finland. Less than a century ago, Finland was a traditional, land-based society. Most people worked at farming, fishing, or forestry. By the end of the twentieth century, only 6 percent of Finns worked the land. Today, Finland is a global leader in technology and is recognized the world over for its innovation and economic progress.

Opposite: **A tourist enjoys a ride on a horse-drawn sled in Lapland.**

Money Facts

Before 2002, the Finnish monetary unit was the *markka*, also called the finnmark. Since 2002, the currency of Finland has been the euro, the common currency of the European Union. One euro is divided into 100 cents. The euro comes in coins worth 1, 2, 5, 10, 20, and 50 cents and 1 and 2 euros. Paper money is issued in values of 5, 10, 20, 50, 100, 200, and 500 euros. In 2008, US$1.00 equaled about 0.63 euros, and 1 euro equaled US$1.58.

Euro coins have a "common side," which represents the EU as a whole, and a "national side," which features a design of a member nation. The common side of each coin shows a map of Europe. Finland's national sides show Finnish symbols. For example, the 2-euro coin shows cloudberries and cloudberry flowers from Lapland, and the 1-euro coin features two flying swans.

On the front of each euro bill is an image of a window or a gateway. On the back is a picture of a bridge. These are not images of actual bridges or windows. Instead, they represent different periods in European history.

This change did not come easily. Particularly hard was an economic depression in Finland in the early 1990s. Finland and the Soviet Union had long been important trading partners, with Finland supplying machinery in exchange for Soviet oil. In 1991, the Soviet Union broke apart into Russia and many smaller nations. The new Russian nation could not continue this trade with Finland, and Finland's manufacturing economy suffered. The number of jobless people in Finland soared. The Finnish government took steps to stabilize the economy, including borrowing money from other nations. Since 1995, the economy of Finland has been growing.

Today, Finland is among the richest nations in the world. Average income for Finns is about US$44,000. Finns enjoy a high standard of living. Ninety-six percent of Finns have televisions and most have satellite TV service. Nearly 70 percent have some kind of video or DVD player. Seventy percent of Finns own cars, and cell phones are everywhere. In 2007, there were more than five million cell phone subscriptions registered in Finland—slightly more than one cell phone per person.

A Nation Built on Trees

Although the forestry industry is not as important as it once was, trees remain a valuable resource in Finland. Most of the timber is cut from forests in central and southeastern Finland. Many of Finland's top companies do something related to trees and timber. Products made from Finland's forests include paper products, plywood, and particleboard. Finland also produces many prefabricated wooden buildings—buildings that are made in factories and then transported in sections to the place where

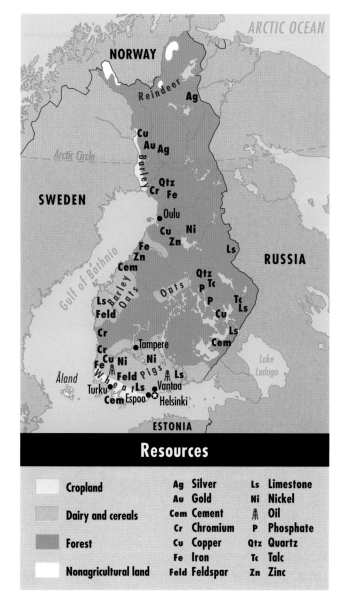

Resources

▢ Cropland	Ag Silver Ls Limestone
	Au Gold Ni Nickel
▨ Dairy and cereals	Cem Cement ⚲ Oil
	Cr Chromium P Phosphate
▮ Forest	Cu Copper Qtz Quartz
	Fe Iron Tc Talc
▢ Nonagricultural land	Feld Feldspar Zn Zinc

they will be erected. Finland exports prefabricated buildings all over the world.

Because of the Finnish expertise in handling lumber and wood, Finns have also become skilled at making the machinery used in the timber industry. Manufacturing this equipment is a large part of Finland's economy. Finish-designed harvesting and papermaking machinery is sold throughout the world, and Finnish experts work as consultants to timber and paper companies in many other countries.

Finland is the second-largest exporter of paper in the world. Most of its paper products are sold in Europe.

What Finland Grows, Makes, and Mines

Agriculture (2006)

Barley	1,972,000 metric tons
Wheat	684,000 metric tons
Rye	51,000 metric tons

Manufacturing (2005, value added in production)

Electrical equipment	US$10,646,000,000
Machinery	US$5,546,000,000
Chemicals	US$5,355,000,000

Mining (2004)

Zinc	37,200 metric tons
Copper	15,500 metric tons
Silver	33 metric tons

Ships are constructed at a Helsinki shipyard. Finland's shipbuilders make many specialty ships such as cruise ships and icebreakers.

Manufacturing

Manufacturing and construction account for about 32 percent of Finland's economy. The nation is a leader in the production of metals and machinery. Finnish manufacturers make mechanical parts for motors and generators, batteries, lightbulbs, telephones, and robots and robotic parts.

Finns are also known for building ships. Living near so much water, Finns have spent hundreds of years perfecting ship design.

Construction of a giant cruise ship is completed at a shipyard in Turku.

Today, Finnish shipyards turn out cruise ships, icebreakers, oil rigs, and small pleasure boats. Other vehicles produced in Finland include farm machinery, such as tractors and harvesters; heavy-duty trucks; and trains.

The chemical industry is also important to the Finnish economy. Finland produces fertilizers, plastics, paints, medicines, and cosmetics.

Hundreds of factories in Finland produce cloth and textiles. Finnish textiles have long had a distinctive look with striking graphic patterns. For a long time, these products were mostly sold within Finland, but people around the world are discovering Finnish textiles. Finns also produce specialty outdoor clothing that is used for skiing, hiking, and other winter pursuits.

Making the Best

Finland is a world leader in design. Innovative Finnish designers aim for functionality, practicality, good looks, and comfort. Finnish design can be seen in everything from household products such as scissors and juicers and linens to more high-tech goods such as cell phones and computers. Graduates of the University of Art and Design in Helsinki are in high demand around the world.

Mining and Agriculture

Zinc, copper, and silver are among Finland's greatest mining resources. Finns also remove chromium, nickel, and gold from the ground. Many of Finland's minerals are used in its metal-manufacturing industries.

Gold is mined in the Lapland region. Gold prices increased in 2003, and many mines in Lapland that had been closed reopened.

Cooperating in Business

Finns' traditional spirit of cooperation sometimes carries over into the business world. Many Finns belong to a kind of business called a cooperative, or co-op. Commonly, businesses belong to private owners or, particularly in communist countries, to the government. Cooperatives, on the other hand, belong to the people who work or shop at the business.

At the beginning of the twentieth century, Finnish farmers founded co-ops as a way to share the costs of buying equipment and getting their goods to market. In cities, people formed co-op supermarkets and other businesses. A co-op buys goods directly from a wholesaler, so co-op members can get goods at lower prices than they would in normal stores. By the middle of the century, a higher percentage of Finns were involved with co-ops than people anywhere else in the Western world. Today, almost 70 percent of Finnish households belong to a consumer co-op.

Agriculture plays only a small part in the Finnish economy. Much of the land is forested, rocky, or swampy, and therefore unsuitable for farming. Today, only about 7 percent of Finnish land is used for agriculture. The main crops are barley, wheat, rye, oats, and sugar beets. Finns also raise cattle, pigs, and sheep.

Most crops in Finland are grown in the coastal lowlands in the southern part of the country.

Many tourists go to Lapland during Christmastime. Tourism is one of the region's primary industries.

At Your Service

Services are the largest part of the Finnish economy. Workers in the service industry include everyone from teachers and doctors to store clerks and ferryboat drivers.

Tourism accounts for a large and growing portion of Finland's economy. In 2005, about four million tourists came to Finland, and the tourism industry contributed about US$10 billion to the Finnish economy. People travel to Finland to experience its gorgeous scenery and enjoy its well-run national parks. Finland has a thriving cruise-ship industry. And in recent years, Finland has seen a rise in tourism around Christmastime, as people travel to Lapland to see reindeer and visit the many Santa Claus villages that have sprung up in the region.

The Nokia Story

The story of Nokia is the story of a company that reinvented itself and grabbed an opportunity to become a leader in a new world of telecommunications. Originally, Nokia was a rubber company. It made rubber for tires, rain boots, and other goods. By the 1970s, the company had branched out into making telephone cables, telegraph cables, and other telecommunications hardware.

In 1982, Nokia made its first mobile phone, then called a "car phone." These were very expensive—they cost several thousand dollars—but they were wildly popular. Nokia continued to refine its designs, making the phones smaller and more portable. At the same time, Nokia helped develop the Global System for Mobile Communications (GSM) network, a communications system that allows cell phones to work around the world. Today, about 80 percent of cell phones use the GSM network.

Technology

In recent years, the telecommunications industry has boomed in Finland. Nokia, the largest manufacturer of cell phones in the world, is also the largest company in Finland. It accounts for about one-third of the value of the Helsinki stock exchange. Dozens of other Finnish companies also do research to provide new and better telecommunications products and services.

Finland has an innovative culture that embraces new technologies and makes the most of them. Each year, the Finnish government gives hundreds of millions of dollars to universities and private companies for research and development of new ideas and technologies. The Finnish government also promotes creative thinking by giving awards to innovative companies. In this way, the government hopes to keep Finland's economy and its people moving forward.

A footbridge leads to the science buildings at Jyvaskyla University. The school is a leader in science and research.

The Finnish People

THE POPULATION OF FINLAND IS FAIRLY HOMOGENEOUS; that is, there is not much ethnic diversity. The five million people of Finland are, for the most part, of Finnish descent.

The Finnish government has designated several groups "national minorities." These tend to be people whose ancestors had roots in Finland during various periods. They include Swedish-speaking Finns (also known as Finland Swedes), the Sámi people, and Romanies (Gypsies).

Opposite: **A man sells flowers, onions, and potatoes at the Helsinki waterfront.**

Most Finns have blonde hair.

Ethnicity in Finland

Finnish	99.0%
Russian	0.4%
Estonian	0.2%
Romany (Gypsy)	0.2%
Sámi	0.1%

*Total does not equal 100% due to rounding.

Traditional Sámi clothing is brightly colored. It is decorated with symbols unique to each family.

The Sámi

The Sámi are one of Finland's few distinct ethnic groups. They have lived in Lapland, the extreme north of Finland, as well as nearby parts of what are now Sweden, Norway, and Russia, for thousands of years. Traditionally, the Sámi were reindeer herders, hunters, and fishers. The Sámi culture was tied to nature, and the people lived close to the land. Today, only a small group of Sámi live this way. Of the approximately 6,500 Sámi in Finland, most live modern lives and hold different kinds of jobs.

Finnish law protects Sámi culture. In 1996, the Sámi Parliament was established. The parliament has twenty-one members who meet to decide on cultural matters and find ways to protect the rights of Sámi-speaking people in larger Finnish society. Today, there are Sámi-language newspapers, radio broadcasts, and television shows.

Romanies

The Romany people are an ethnic group that is spread across Europe and elsewhere around the world. Also known as Gypsies, Romanies were traditionally nomadic, moving from place to place. They first arrived in Finland in the 1500s. Today, Finland is home to about ten thousand Romanies, most of whom live in or near Helsinki. Romanies in Finland tend to have more trouble finding jobs than other Finns, and their housing is often poor. Many Romanies continue to wear their traditional dress—large, colorful skirts for women and dark suits for men.

Teenage Romany girls wear traditional clothing in a Finnish shopping center.

Population of Major Cities (2006 est.)	
Helsinki	564,521
Espoo	235,019
Tampere	206,638
Vantaa	189,711
Turku	175,354
Oulu	130,178

Somalis are the largest non-European immigrant group in Finland.

Throughout history, the number of immigrants in Finland has been low. But in recent years, Finland has begun attracting more immigrants. In 1980, only 12,800 foreigners lived in Finland. Most were from Sweden, Germany, the United States, and the Soviet Union. By 1990, the number of foreigners living in Finland had risen to 26,200, but most were still Swedes. As of 2002, 152,000 foreigners lived in Finland. Russians are now the largest immigrant group, followed by Estonians, Swedes, and Somalis.

The first Somalis came to Finland in 1991 as political refugees. Many had been students in Soviet universities. They fled to Finland to avoid returning to their East African nation, which was racked by violence. Soon, more Somalis joined them. Many were family members trying to stay together. Today, Finland is home to about 9,000 Somalis.

From Country to City

As recently as the end of World War II, most people in Finland lived in rural areas. Today, about 80 percent live in urban areas, with almost one-fifth of of the country's population residing in or around Helsinki. This shows

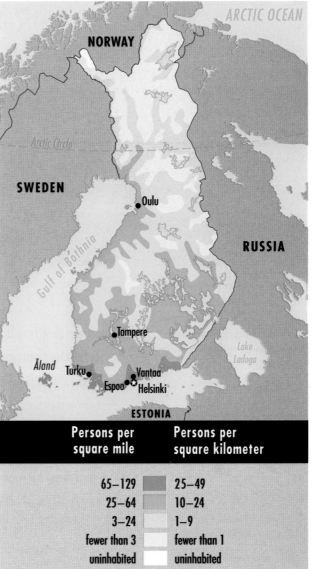

Persons per square mile		Persons per square kilometer
65–129		25–49
25–64		10–24
3–24		1–9
fewer than 3		fewer than 1
uninhabited		uninhabited

the changing nature of work in Finland. Jobs in agriculture and forestry have dwindled, while the market for more urban-based work in technology, engineering, and manufacturing is booming.

Above left: **A welder works at a shipyard in Helsinki.**

The Finnish People **89**

Students conduct a science experiment at Tammerkosken Lukio High School. The school has a challenging curriculum that prepares students for college.

The School System

Finland prides itself on its excellent education system. Finnish schoolchildren routinely score among the highest in the world in reading, math, and science tests.

Some children start preschool at age five, but they are not required to attend school until age seven. They must continue until age sixteen. The children are taught in either Finnish or Swedish, depending on what they speak at home. Children learn math, history, geography, literature, civics, environmental science, music, art, physical education, and at least three languages—Finnish, Swedish, and English. A single classroom teacher teaches most of the subjects. This basic schooling is called comprehensive school.

Once teenagers complete comprehensive school, they have a choice—vocational school or secondary school. Vocational programs last for two to five years and train students for jobs in the workforce. Secondary school, which lasts three years, prepares students to go on to college. Students take entrance exams before being admitted to a college or university. Entrance to Finnish universities is competitive. Not everyone who takes or even passes an entrance exam gains admittance to a university. Finland's largest university is the University of Helsinki.

Many Finns take advantage of their nation's extensive adult education system. Some people simply take classes for fun. Others want to learn a new trade. If a Finn becomes unemployed or is in a field that is changing, he or she can go back to school—free of charge—to learn a new career. Finns credit their education system for their strong economy and high standard of living.

The Helsinki University of Technology is located in Otaniemi, a district in the city of Espoo. Finnish architect Alvar Aalto designed the main building.

A Lonely Language

Finns speak a language that has a mysterious history. Most European languages belong to the giant Indo-European language family. But Finnish belongs to a separate, much smaller family of languages called Finno-Ugrian.

Only two other Finno-Ugric languages have significant numbers of speakers. Estonian, spoken in the country of Estonia, just across the Gulf of Finland from Helsinki, is a close cousin of Finnish. Speakers of the two languages can usually understand each other. That's not true of the more distantly related Hungarian language, spoken farther south in Europe, in Hungary. Like long-lost relatives, Hungarian and Finnish have distant family resemblances, but their speakers would find words in the other language unfamiliar.

The roots of the Finno-Ugric languages are mysterious. At one time, researchers suggested links to languages of faraway Mongolia, near China, or to the long-ago lost language of the Etruscans, people who lived in areas of Italy in ancient times. Few today believe those theories, but people do agree that Finnish is a very unusual language.

The Languages of Finland

The biggest distinction among Finns is in which language they speak. Swedish was the official language of Finland for hundreds of years until the late nineteenth century. Today, Finland has two official languages—Finnish and Swedish—and they have equal status. Both languages are used in government documents, on television, and in radio.

About 93 percent of Finns speak Finnish, and about 5 percent speak Swedish. In school, children begin their studies in either Finnish or Swedish but eventually learn both languages. A small number of people in Finland speak Sámi or Russian as their first language.

Speaking Finnish

Finnish is one of the official languages of Finland. It is also a minority language in Norway and

Pronouncing Finnish

All Finnish words have the stress on the first syllable. Here are some other differences between Finnish and English:

Letter	Pronunciation
h	always hard, as in "head"
ng	soft, as in "singer"
r	always rolled
j	like *y* in "yellow"
ä	like *a* in "cat"
ää	stretch out the ä sound
ö	like *er* in "number"
öö	stretch out the ö sound

Sweden. Unlike other Scandinavian languages, Finnish does not belong to the Indo-European language family. Instead, it is part of the Finno-Ugric language family, as are Hungarian and Estonian.

Finnish has a reputation among English speakers as being difficult to learn. Nouns in Finnish can have any of 15 different endings, and verbs have as many as 160 different forms. Finnish words are easy to spell and pronounce, however, as each letter makes only one sound, and no letters are silent.

Finnish periodicals are displayed at a newsstand in Helsinki.

How Do You Say . . . ?	
hello	*hei* (hay)
good-bye	*näkemiin* (NA-ke-meen)
thank you	*kiitos* (KEE-tohs)
yes	*kyllä* (KUUL-la)
no	*ei* (ay)
How are you?	*Mitä kuuluu?* (MEE-ta KOO-loo?)
Fine, thank you	*Kiitos, hyvää* (KEE-toss, HUU-vaa)
Nice to meet you	*Hauska tavata* (HOWS-kah TAH-vah-tah)
I can't speak Finnish.	*En puhu suomea.* (EN POO-hoo SOO-oh-meh-ah)

Spiritual Life

R ELIGION FIGURES STRONGLY IN THE LIVES OF MOST Finns. Most are baptized, confirmed, married, and buried in church. But few attend church on a regular basis. The only time churches fill up is at Christmas. Instead, Finns tend to be private about their religious observance. Only 14 percent of Finns attend church services at least once a month, but 75 percent say they pray sometimes.

Opposite: **The green dome of the Lutheran Cathedral dominates Helsinki's skyline.**

Temppeliaukio Church is known as the Church of the Rock because it was built into solid rock.

Naming Celebrations

Most parents in Finland name their babies when they have them baptized, at about two months of age. It is traditional to keep the baby's name a secret until this christening. Many Finns receive two first names. One of their first names runs in the family, and the other is the name of a saint. By custom, people celebrate their saint's name day in Finland. It is almost like a birthday celebration, with cards and well-wishing. Finnish adults also bring candy to work to celebrate a saint's name day.

Today, about 84 percent of Finns belong to the Evangelical Lutheran Church. About 2 percent belong to other Christian groups, including the Orthodox, Pentacostal, and Roman Catholic churches. The number of Muslims is small but growing due to immigration. About 13.5 percent of Finns do not practice any religion.

Uspenski Cathedral in Helsinki is the main cathedral of the Orthodox Church of Finland.

Turku Cathedral was built more than seven hundred years ago.

Church and State

The history of Finland is intertwined with the history of religion in Europe. Christianity came to Finland by the early twelfth century. Both the Roman Catholic Church and the Orthodox Church, separate branches of Christianity, sent missionaries to Finland to spread their faith.

Finland's move to Lutheranism came in the sixteenth century, when King Gustavus Vasa of Sweden, who then ruled Finland, joined the Protestant Reformation. At that time, the Lutheran Church became the official church of Finland. The government gave money to and also regulated the Lutheran Church in Finland. The church, meanwhile, largely took charge of local governments and education. In 1548, Mikael Agricola, who would later become the first Lutheran bishop of Finland, translated part of the Bible into Finnish. Before this, few Finns had been able to read the holy book of their religion.

Religion in Finland

Evangelical Lutheran	84.2%
Finnish Orthodox	1.1%
Other Christian	1.1%
Other	0.1%
None	13.5%

Bringing Religion to the People

Mikael Agricola was born in 1510 in southeastern Finland to a well-off family of farmers. He was a good student, and the path for good students at that time led to the priesthood. His studies landed him in Turku, which was then the capital of Swedish-ruled Finland. He began working for Martii Skytte, the bishop of Turku, and was ordained as a priest in 1531.

In Turku, Agricola met some followers of Martin Luther, a German priest who believed that the Roman Catholic Church had grown corrupt. Luther and his followers broke away from the Catholic Church and began the Protestant Reformation. Skytte was also a follower of Luther's. He started to implement some of Luther's ideas, including saying mass in Finnish and Swedish instead of in Latin, as the Catholic Church demanded.

Under Skytte's guidance, Agricola began the first translation of the Bible into Finnish. While teaching at the Turku Cathedral School, he wrote *Abckiria*, the first Finnish-language schoolbook. He then wrote *Rucouskiria*, a book of prayer and writings about the Reformation. His most important work was his translation of the New Testament, which he finished in 1548.

Finnish speakers could now read part of the Bible and learn to pray in their own language.

Agricola was appointed bishop of Turku in 1554, making him the first Lutheran bishop of Finland. He died in 1557, before he could finish translating the entire Bible into Finnish. Agricola ignited a nationalist movement that grew over several hundred years and eventually led to Finnish independence.

After Russia gained power in Finland in the nineteenth century, the Finnish Orthodox Church also became an official church in Finland. Finns had to belong to either the Finnish Lutheran Church or the Finnish Orthodox Church until 1899. Beginning that year, other Protestant churches were made legal.

Freedom of Religion

In 1923, Finns passed the Freedom of Religion Act, allowing people to belong to any religion or no religion.

Today, Finnish law guarantees freedom of religion and conscience. Children in Finland receive religious instruction in school according to their own religious beliefs. Religion is not practiced in school. Instead, it is studied like any other subject. Students learn about the history and cultural significance of religion and talk about ethics. Students who do not belong to any religion take a course of ethics and cultural study.

In 2006, the Jewish community of Helsinki celebrated the one hundredth anniversary of the construction of Helsinki Synagogue.

People had lived in what is now Finland for thousands of years before Christian missionaries arrived. These people had their own religion, which was closely tied to nature and the world around them. The early Finns worshipped many gods, including Ukko, the supreme god of sky, crops, thunder, and lightning (*ukkonen* is the modern Finnish word for "thunderstorm"). Ukko's wife, Akka, was the mother earth goddess. Other gods included Ahti, the god of the sea and fishing, and his wife, Vellamo, who is often pictured as a mermaid. Tapio and Tellervo were the god and goddess of the woods, and Sampso was the god of seeds and planting.

The spirit world contained other beings as well. Spirits called *haltijas* could take many forms. Sometimes they looked like humans. Other times they looked like animals. Each village or tribe had its own haltija, which the community worshipped. Buildings and families had their own haltijas as well, which were supposed to protect them and bring prosperity. Families typically had a place where they made sacrifices of food or silver to keep the haltijas happy.

Elements of nature were also thought to have spirits. The people believed there were spirits in the air, in the water, in the woods. They thought that the spirits could bring good luck or bad, depending on their mood. Shamans,

In the traditional Sámi religion, people used drums to communicate with the spirit world. Today, Christianity is widespread among the Sámi.

Sacred Animals in Finnish Culture

Many of the animals that are closely associated with Finland today have been important to the Finnish people throughout history. In the days before Christianity reached Finland, several animals had important religious significance.

Ancient Finns believed that bears came from the sky and could be reborn after death. In one ceremony, they sacrificed a bear for a feast. After killing the bear, they honored it. They buried the bones and placed the skull high in a sacred tree, in hopes that the bear could return to the sky and then come back to earth.

Birds in general were holy to the ancient Finns, who believed that a bird created the world. Some told a story of the world coming from a bird's egg. Others said the earth was formed from mud scooped up in the beak of a bird. The Karelians, one of the country's ancient tribes, believed that a bird brings a soul to a newborn baby, and the same bird returns to take the soul back when the person dies. This "soul-bird" was carved on many tombstones in Finland.

The swan was particularly sacred to ancient Finns. People thought that the swan's long neck allowed it to see to the world of the spirits. Some people believed that if you killed a swan, you would die soon after.

people with a special relationship with the spirit world, tried to communicate with the spirits, asking them to cure the sick and help crops to grow.

Arts and Sports

THE ARTS ARE A REGULAR PART OF FINNISH LIFE. FINNS GO to concerts and the theater. They read, they listen, they write.

Literature is at the center of Finnish culture. More books per person are published in Finland than in any other nation. Finns also make great use of public libraries. Not surprisingly, then, the government supports writers with grants and prizes in order to encourage the creation of Finnish literature.

Opposite: **The monument to composer Jean Sibelius is in Helsinki. It is made of steel tubing.**

A woman reads in a library in Helsinki.

Finnish literature is said to have started with the publication of the *Kalevala*, the national epic poem. The *Kalevala* was written by Elias Lönnrot, a country doctor who had an interest in folk songs and stories. Lönnrot collected the stories he heard in rural villages and eventually put them all together in one epic, or grand, poem, which was published in 1835. The *Kalevala* tells the story of Väinämöinen, a hero who has magical powers. Through the various stories, Väinämöinen

A series of sculptures featuring characters from the *Kalevala* adorn a building in Helsinki. In this one, Väinämöinen plays a traditional Finnish stringed instrument.

and other characters face and overcome hardships—struggles like those of the Finnish people, who were starting to wish for freedom.

The *Kalevala* collected and wove together a long tradition of Finnish folktales and songs. Some of these might have been lost had it not been for Lönnrot. The epic was the first work of literature to be written and published in Finnish. At the time, Finland was still a territory of Sweden, and all literature was written in Swedish. To this day, the *Kalevala* stands as a masterpiece of Finnish culture.

The first Finnish-language novel, published in 1870, was *Seven Brothers*, by Aleksis Kivi. Generally considered one of the greatest works of Finnish literature, the story concerns brothers who want to live simply off the land. But society pressures them to become educated and civilized. *Tales of the Ensign Ståhl* is a collection of poems written in Swedish by Johan Ludvig Runeberg. The collection includes the poem "Our Land," which is now the unofficial Finnish national anthem.

Finnish literature flourished in the early twentieth century. Frans Eemil Sillanpaa won the Nobel Prize for Literature in 1939. His works such as *Meek Heritage* and *The Maid Silja* brought to life the struggles of the poor of Finland. Another

Johan Ludvig Runeberg lived from 1804 to 1877. He is considered Finland's national poet.

Moominworld

Finland's most beloved children's characters are the Moomins. The Moomins were created by writer and illustrator Tove Jansson (1914–2001). She wrote dozens of books about the Moomin family—Moominmamma, Moominpappa, and their son, Moomintroll. They live in a blue Moominhouse in a town called Moominvalley. They have many adventures but are always kind and tolerant of different kinds of creatures they encounter.

The Moomins started as one book and took off from there. Today, the Moomins come to life in books, comics, and films. The Moomin stories have been translated into more than thirty languages.

The Moomins have their own theme park, Moominworld, in Naantali near Turku. It's a hands-on place with little glitz and glamour and no rides. The main attraction is the big blue Moominhouse, which children can explore. The park also includes replicas of other parts of the Moomins' world, including Moominpappa's boat, Moominmamma's donut factory, and, of course, the Moomins themselves.

classic Finnish novel is *The Unknown Soldier,* by Vaino Linna, which looks at World War II from the point of view of an ordinary soldier. In the 1940s, Tove Jansson began writing children's books about a family of creatures called the Moomins. The Moomin books have been more widely translated than almost any other Finnish books.

Finns love all kinds of music. They listen to classical and jazz music, to rap, and to modern rock.

The greatest Finnish classical composer, Jean Sibelius, was born in 1865. He composed eight symphonies and a handful of shorter works. Sibelius had been raised by nationalist parents and sent to a Finnish-language school. Nationalism and love of Finland were a large part of his music. Sibelius died in 1957. The people of Finland so loved him that a huge monument to him was built in Helsinki. It is an enormous grouping of metal tubes that resemble the pipes of an organ.

Classical music is still popular in Finland today. Many young Finnish composers continue to write symphonies and operas. The nation has more than thirty professional orchestras, and dozens of annual music festivals showcase new works.

Finns like pop music too. Metal and hard rock bands are popular, and a few have gained success outside of Finland. In 2006, the Finnish band Lordi won the Eurovision Song Contest, an annual international pop music contest for bands from all over Europe.

Composer Jean Sibelius studied and later taught at the Music Institute of Helsinki.

Care to Tango?

Finland has for a century embraced the tango, a dance that comes from Argentina, halfway around the world. The tango fad brought the sounds of South America to Europe in the early twentieth century. By the 1930s, the first Finnish-composed tangos rang out from bandstands across the country. The music and dance form hit new heights of popularity with Finns during World War II, and a serious revival has been underway since the 1980s. In 1984, an annual tango festival began in the town of Seinäjoki. The Tangomarkkinat, as the festival is called, now runs five days and attracts one hundred thousand people.

Dance

Finland has a tradition of folk dance that goes back centuries. The Finnish Folklore Association trains folk-dancing teachers, who then teach at local clubs.

Finland also has a national ballet and a thriving modern dance and independent dance scene.

Spectators watch as dancers in traditional clothing perform folk dances at Midsummer festivities in Helsinki.

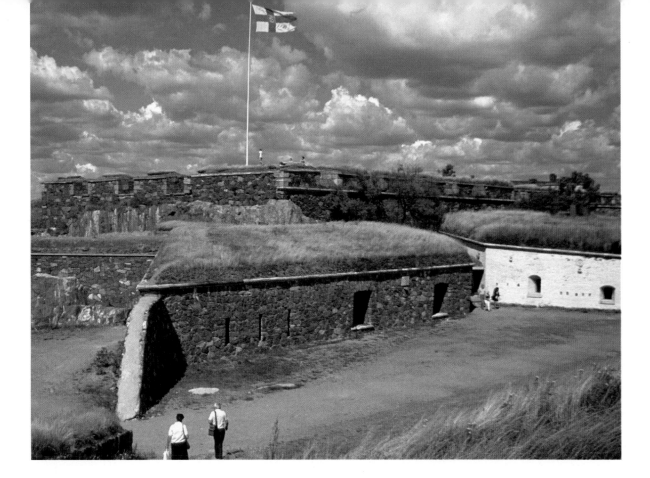

Finns also like to dance for fun. Young people fill dance clubs, and the tango, a dance that originated in Argentina, is hugely popular.

In the summer, the fort at Suomenlinna is a popular tourist destination and outdoor theater.

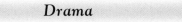
Drama

Finland boasts a lively theater world, with about sixty theater companies. Half of all Finns go to the theater at least once a year. In the summer, many communities put on plays in unusual outdoor venues. Turku has a theater at the foot of an old mill. An ancient fort on the island of Suomenlinna is home to a summer-theater group. At the Pyynikki summer theater, the audience sits on a turntable that revolves around the stage.

Eliel Saarinen designed the Helsinki Central Railway Station. The granite structure was completed in 1919.

Art and Architecture

Finland has made huge contributions to the world in the areas of architecture and design. Finns have been designing and building beautiful buildings since the Middle Ages. An early example is the Church of St. Olaf in the Åland Islands, one of the oldest churches in Finland, which dates to 1280.

In the twentieth century, several Finnish architects became world renowned. In 1914, Eliel Saarinen drew attention for the bold lines of his Helsinki Central Railway Station. In a nod to Finnish tradition, Alvar Aalto designed simple, elegant buildings that used a great deal of wood. Aalto also designed furniture and glassware. The Aalto vase, also called the wave vase, has a curvy glass shape the architect and designer perfected with his wife, Aino, who was also an architect.

Finnish handicrafts also show a strong sense of design. Artisans create beautiful pieces that reflect the Finnish connection to nature. Finnish designers excel at using natural materials, such as wood and glass, to create beautiful and functional objects. The Marimekko label is known for bold textile designs, while the Arabia company's pottery sells well around the world.

The bold designs of Marimekko are displayed at the Design Museum in Helsinki.

Finns love sports. They love watching them, and they love playing them. They love the slap of a hockey stick and the roar of a race car. Formula One car racing is a top spectator sport in Finland. Motocross and motorcycle racing are also popular.

More than 90 percent of Finns say they get regular physical exercise. Finnish children take physical education class at school, and 40 percent of them also participate in organized sports outside of school. Finns of all ages play soccer, hockey, and a game called floorball, which is a bit like floor hockey. Running and swimming are also popular.

Since the late 1990s, hundreds of thousands of Finns have taken up Nordic walking. Nordic walking is walking with two sticks that are similar to ski poles. In fact, Nordic walking began as a way for skiers to stay in shape in the summer.

The Flying Finns

In 1912, a Finnish runner named Hannes Kolehmainen won three gold medals in the Olympics. He was nicknamed the Flying Finn. After that, Finns dominated the world of long-distance running, and people used the name Flying Finn to describe all successful Finnish runners. These include Paavo Nurmi, who won eight gold medals in the Olympics in 1920 and 1924, and Lasse Viren, who won two events in the 1972 and 1976 Olympics.

Finns no longer dominate running, but the nickname Flying Finn is still in use. Finland's top race-car drivers—Keke Rosberg, Mika Häkkinen, and Kimi Räikkönen—are today's Flying Finns.

Many Finns enjoy cross-country skiing.

Of course, winter sports are popular in Finland. Finns say they need something fun to do during the long winter months. A specific skiing vacation is even built into the school calendar! There are not many mountains in Finland, but Lapland has a few, so Finns go there for downhill skiing. Cross-country skiing is popular everywhere else. Some Finns also train to become ski jumpers. In this sport, skiers race down a ramp and soar off the end, trying to fly as far as possible.

Finnish Baseball

The national sport of Finland is *pesäpallo*, also called "Finnish baseball." The game is based on American baseball. There are a home base and three other bases. Players hit a ball with a bat and then try to run around the bases. One difference between the two sports is that in pesäpallo the bases are not laid out in a diamond. Instead, they are in a zigzag pattern like a backward Z. Pesäpallo is also played outside of Finland. The country competes against Australia, Germany, and Sweden in a championship each year.

Life as a Finn

THE FINNISH PEOPLE HAVE ONE OF THE HIGHEST STANdards of living in the world. Crime rates are low, and most Finns enjoy freedom and prosperity. The government pays for health care and more than a year of parental leave after a baby is born. This comes at a cost, however. Finns pay a large portion of their salaries to the government in taxes. But Finns will say that what they get back in return is worth it.

Opposite: **A child reads in a library in Helsinki.**

People buy food, flowers, and other items in the Market Square in Helsinki.

Dogs of Finland

The early Finns were hunters and farmers who lived close to the land. They domesticated three breeds of dogs to help them in their work. These breeds are still found in Finland today.

The Finnish spitz (left), the Karelian bear dog (right), and the Nordic spitz are all hunting dogs, though they were bred for different purposes. The Finnish spitz is a "bark pointer." Its barking causes birds to fly up so hunters can shoot at them. The Finnish spitz is a small but fearless dog.

The Karelian Bear Dog is used to hunt elk, wild boar, and moose, though it will also attack a bear, as the name suggests. The Nordic spitz is an all-purpose hunting dog used for tracking small prey.

The Finnish Family

The average Finnish family has two working parents and two children, but that is changing. Many families now have one or no children.

Finns are given long parental leave, or time off, from work to stay home to care for a young baby. It is not unusual for a Finnish mother to have one or two years off from her job—with

Women at Work

Finnish women are better educated and better employed than women in most other parts of the world. Today, almost all Finnish women work outside the home. But that doesn't mean everything is equal between men and women. Women in Finland are more likely to work in lower-paying industries and less likely to hold leadership positions in business. As for salary, women in Finland are paid, on average, only 80 percent of what men are paid for doing jobs in the same fields—even though women tend to be better educated than men.

an allowance—when a baby is born. Preschool-aged children are guaranteed a low-cost spot in a local daycare center. This makes it possible for parents to return to work more easily.

A mother and daughter enjoy a day in the park.

Maternity Pack

When a baby is born in Finland, the parents have a choice. They can either take a cash payment from the government to buy things the baby will need, or they can receive a "maternity pack" from the government. The maternity pack has clothes, toys, diapers, and everything else they will need to care for the baby.

Housing

About half of Finns live in single-family houses. The rest live in apartment buildings or townhouses. All Finnish homes are well built and well insulated against the brutally cold winters. Just about every Finnish home has a sauna, a traditional Finnish steam bath.

Apartment buildings are common in Finnish cities and suburbs.

Although most Finns now live in a city or a town, many try to get to the country as often as possible. A Finnish tradition is the summerhouse. Many Finnish families own or rent a house or cottage in the country where they go for part or all of the summer. People in Finland commonly have the whole month of July off from work. They pack up and move to the summerhouse. At other times, families travel to the summerhouse for weekends. Families hike and pick berries and use the sauna and generally just relax and have a good time.

Many Finnish families have country houses. This traditional country house is near Kannuskoski, in southern Finland.

Getting Around

About 70 percent of Finns own cars, and they pride themselves on being good drivers. Bicycling is also popular. Most Finns also own a bicycle, and they ride it all year, even in winter. Most towns and cities have good bike paths for safe and easy biking.

Hundreds of bikes are parked outside the Helsinki Central Railway Station.

A program called Citybikes allows people to borrow bikes easily. At bike stands around Helsinki, a person pays a small deposit, borrows a bike, and then returns it to any of the bike stands when he or she is done.

Media

Finland has a reputation as a country that values information and news. Although Finland has only five million people, it boasts about two hundred newspapers, more than two thousand magazines, dozens of commercial radio stations, three digital radio channels, and four national TV channels. About 80 percent of Finns read a newspaper daily. The average Finn reads twelve magazines regularly. The most popular newspaper in Finland is *Helsingin Sanomat*, with more than four hundred thousand subscribers.

Classic Cakes

Two popular desserts in Finland take their names from historical figures. Runeberg cake is a jam-topped spice cake that honors the Finnish national poet, Johan Ludvig Runeberg. Runeberg wrote the poem that became the unofficial Finnish national anthem. It is traditional to eat Runeberg cake on his birthday, February 5.

The Alexander cake is a flat rectangular cake with a layer of mixed apple and raspberry jam, topped with pink glaze. It is named for the Russian emperor Alexander I.

Eating Like a Finn

Traditionally, Finnish food was hearty because the Finns had physical jobs and lived in a harsh climate. Filling foods gave them the energy to work hard and keep warm. Most Finns now work indoors, in offices, stores, and schools. Since their jobs have changed, Finns do not need to eat so much, but they have kept some of their traditional diet.

Bread with tomatoes and cucumbers is a common light meal in Finland.

Pea Soup Thursdays

In Finland, Thursday is pea soup day. Every week, all over the country, all workplace and school cafeterias serve pea soup on Thursdays. Many people who do not eat in cafeterias make the soup at home on Thursdays. The traditional dessert that follows pea soup is crepes with jam.

Bread is a staple, or regular part, of the Finnish diet. Finnish bread is usually made of rye instead of wheat, the commonly used grain in breads of many other countries. Finns eat tons of both rye crispbread, which is crunchy and hard, and soft, fresh-baked rye bread. Finns also eat a lot of meat, especially pork and beef. Meatballs are common, as are ground meat and sausage. Fish also plays a large role in the Finnish diet.

Ruisleipä is kind of bread made in a ring shape. Traditionally, loaves were stored on poles under farmhouse ceilings.

Salmon, herring, perch, and whitefish are all popular. Finns often use smoke to cook their fish. Finns make many fine cheeses, including Emmentaler and blue cheese. They also drink a lot of milk and a lot of coffee. In fact, Finns drink more coffee than any other people in the world.

Fish are smoked on a grill. Many summer vacationers like to smoke the fish that they have caught.

Vegetables and fruits are not a mainstay of the Finnish diet because the growing season is short and imported produce is expensive. The Finns do eat lots of wild berries and mushrooms, however.

A typical breakfast in Finland includes coffee, bread, and oatmeal or muesli (a mixture of uncooked oats, dried fruit, and nuts). Many Finns have their main meal at lunchtime. Hot meals are served in all schools and at many workplaces. Lunch includes meat or fish, more bread, vegetables such as cabbage, and sometimes dessert. In the cold winter months, the noontime meal is hearty and warm. The evening meal can be fairly light, sometimes just a snack.

Delicious Desserts

Like people all over the world, Finns like their desserts. Here are some popular ones:

pulla – a spicy yeast bread, often served with coffee

pasha – a cheesecake, served at Easter and decorated with Easter symbols

tippaleipä – fried crullers (twisted sweet cakes) served on the first day of May

laskiaispulla – buns filled with almond paste and whipped cream

crepes – thin pancakes, usually filled with berry jam

mignon eggs – real eggshells filled with chocolate—an Easter treat

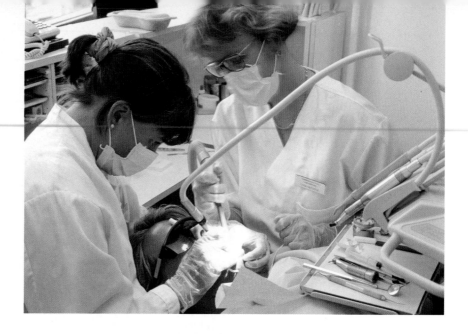

A Helsinki dentist and her assistant work on a patient's teeth.

Health Care for All

Finland has a national health insurance program that provides health care to all citizens. Everyone can go to doctors and medical centers for check-ups, emergency care, laboratory tests, X-rays, and other hospital services. Many of these services are free. Patients never have to pay more than a small portion of the bill. Finns can choose to pay for private health care in addition to what the government provides.

Children also get regular checkups and vaccinations at school. Health care teams closely monitor Finnish children at their schools, with an eye toward preventing diseases and keeping children healthy.

The health system provides specialized care as well. Care at home or at nursing homes, rehabilitation, physical therapy, and dental treatment are all included. Disabled Finns are entitled to special services like housing, special accommodations at work, training, interpretation for the deaf, and guide dogs for the blind.

Holidays

Traditionally, Finns fly the flag from sunrise to sunset on public holidays. They celebrate some holidays such as New Year's Day and Easter in much the way people in other parts of the world do. But some holidays have special customs in Finland.

May Day, May 1, marks the coming of summer. This holiday honors workers, graduating students, and the end of spring, all in one day. People begin celebrating the night before, with parties all over town. Many Finns wear their white graduation caps on May 1, even if they aren't new graduates. Meanwhile, political organizations and trade unions organize rallies on May Day, which is Labor Day in Europe.

Midsummer's Day, which marks the longest day of the year, is one of the biggest holidays in Finland. Midsummer is celebrated on the closest Saturday to June 21. Many people head for the country for Midsummer's Day. There they have big parties with bonfires and lots of food and dancing. In some parts of Finland, the sun doesn't set on Midsummer's Day, so celebrations can last all night or even all weekend. People also fly the Finnish flag all night long.

National Holidays

New Year's Day	January 1
Epiphany	January 6
Easter	March or April
Pentecost	May
May Day	May 1
Midsummer's Day	around June 21
All Saints Day	November 1
Independence Day	December 6
Christmas	December 25

Finns have bonfires to celebrate Midsummer's Day.

Finland seems to have been made for Christmas. It's said that Santa Claus lives in Lapland, the place where reindeer make their home. Families celebrate Christmas on December 24 with an evening meal and then a visit from Santa Claus. Santa comes to the door when the children are still awake and asks, "Are there well-behaved children here?" He leaves gifts when he is assured the children have been good. Finnish families often visit graveyards on Christmas Eve to light candles on the graves of loved ones. Christmas Day is a quiet day for relaxing. The day after Christmas is a time for parties.

Shoppers browse the stalls at the Christmas market in Rovaniemi.

The Sauna

The sauna is an old Finnish tradition. Saunas have been used in Finland for about two thousand years. The word *sauna* means "steam bath," and a sauna is just that—a wooden building or room where stones are heated until they are hot. Bathers then throw water on the hot stones to create steam in the room. The temperature in a sauna is between 170 and 200°F (75 and 95°C). This is sweltering, but the point is to sweat.

A sauna is much more than just a steam bath to Finns. It's a social event. It's a family bonding activity. It's a vital part of Finnish culture. Just about every Finnish home has a sauna, as do many businesses. Finns use saunas as a chance to chat and catch up with friends and family.

To take a sauna like a Finn, you sit in the steam for a while, perhaps patting your skin with small birch branches. After a while in the steam, you will want to cool down. With many modern saunas, that means taking a cold shower, but a jump into a cool country lake is even better. After drying off and dressing, you go for a snack with friends and family.

A Place Like No Other

Finland is a place of contrasts. It is a place where people love both classical and metal music. It is a place where reindeer roam but everyone owns a cell phone. It is a place where the church is important but spirituality is private. It is a place where people work hard and play hard. It is a place of *sisu* and *talkoot*. It is Finland.

Timeline

Finland History		World History	
People first settle in Finland.	8500 B.C.		
		2500 B.C.	Egyptians build the pyramids and the Sphinx in Giza.
		563 B.C.	The Buddha is born in India.
		A.D. 313	The Roman emperor Constantine legalizes Christianity.
		610	The Prophet Muhammad begins preaching a new religion called Islam.
Sweden and Novgorod send missionaries to Finland.	A.D. 1050		
		1054	The Eastern (Orthodox) and Western (Roman Catholic) Churches break apart.
		1095	The Crusades begin.
		1215	King John seals the Magna Carta.
Turku Castle is built.	1280		
A treaty between Sweden and Novogorod divides Karelia.	1323	1300s	The Renaissance begins in Italy.
Finland becomes part of the Kingdom of Denmark.	1397	1347	The plague sweeps through Europe.
		1453	Ottoman Turks capture Constantinople, conquering the Byzantine Empire.
		1492	Columbus arrives in North America.
Sweden-Finland breaks free from Denmark under King Gustavus Vasa.	1523	1500s	Reformers break away from the Catholic Church, and Protestantism is born.
Mikael Agricola translates part of the Bible into Finnish, sparking interest in the Finnish language.	1548		
Sweden cedes part of Finland to Russia at the end of the Great Northern War.	1721	1776	The U.S. Declaration of Independence is signed.

Finland History

Sweden surrenders Finland to Russia.	1809
Saimaa Canal opens.	1856
Finland becomes the first European country to allow women to vote.	1906
Finland becomes an independent nation.	1917
Finland adopts a national constitution; Kaarlo Juho Ståhlberg is elected its the first president.	1919
The Soviet Union defeats Finland in the Winter War.	1939–1940
The Soviet Union defeats Finland in the Continuation War.	1941–1944
The Summer Olympics are held in Helsinki.	1952
Urho Kaleva Kekkonen is elected president for the first time.	1956
A severe economic depression strikes Finland.	early 1990s
Finland joins the European Union.	1995
Tarja Halonen is elected the first female president of Finland.	2000
Finland begins using the euro as its unit of currency.	2002
President Halonen wins reelection.	2006

World History

1789	The French Revolution begins.
1865	The American Civil War ends.
1879	The first practical lightbulb is invented.
1914	World War I begins.
1917	The Bolshevik Revolution brings communism to Russia.
1929	A worldwide economic depression begins.
1939	World War II begins.
1945	World War II ends.
1957	The Vietnam War begins.
1969	Humans land on the Moon.
1975	The Vietnam War ends.
1989	The Berlin Wall is torn down as communism crumbles in Eastern Europe.
1991	The Soviet Union breaks into separate countries.
2001	Terrorists attack the World Trade Center in New York City and the Pentagon in Arlington, Virginia.

Fast Facts

Official name: Republic of Finland

Capital: Helsinki

Official languages: Finnish and Swedish

Helsinki

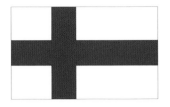

Finland's flag

Birch trees

National anthem:	"Maame" in Finnish, "Vårt Land" in Swedish ("Our Land")
Government:	Multiparty republic
Chief of state:	President
Head of government:	Prime minister
Area:	130,559 square miles (338,145 square km)
Greatest distance north to south:	717 miles (1,154 km)
Greatest distance east to west:	336 (541 km)
Bordering countries:	Norway to the north, Russia to the east, and Sweden to the northwest
Highest elevation:	Mount Haltia, 4,356 feet (1,328 m)
Lowest elevation:	Sea level, along the coast
Average high temperatures:	In Helsinki, 72°F (22°C) in July; 27°F (–3°C) in January
Average low temperatures:	In Helsinki, 55°F (13°C) in July; 16°F (–9°C) in January
Average annual precipitation:	27 inches (69 cm)
National population (2007 est.):	5,238,460

Turku Castle

Population of largest cities (2006 est.):

Helsinki	564,521
Espoo	235,019
Tampere	206,638
Vantaa	189,711
Turku	175,354

Famous landmarks:
- ▶ *Ateneum Art Museum*, Helsinki
- ▶ *Church of St. Olaf*, Åland Islands
- ▶ *Lutheran Cathedral*, Helsinki
- ▶ *Lemmenjoki*, Lapland
- ▶ *National Museum of Finland*, Helsinki
- ▶ *Turku Castle*, Turku

Industry: The timber industry has long been important to Finland. The country also has a strong manufacturing sector producing electrical equipment, machinery, chemicals, wood products, metals, textiles, and ships. Finland is a leader in the fields of design and telecommunications. Major mining products include zinc, copper, and silver. Agriculture plays only a small role in Finland's economy. The main agricultural products are barley, wheat, rye, oats, and sugar beets.

Currency: The euro; in 2008, US$1 equaled about 0.63 euros, and 1 euro equaled US$1.58.

Weights and measures: The metric system

Literacy rate: 100%

Currency

High school students

Urho Kaleva Kekkonen

Common Finnish words and phrases:

Kylla	Yes
Ei	No
Hei	Hello
Näkemiin	Good-bye
Anteeksi	Excuse me
Olkaa hyvä	Please
Kiitos	Thank you
Olkaa hyvä	You're welcome.
Olen pahoillani	I'm sorry.
Mika sinun nimesi on?	What is your name?

Famous Finns:

Alvar Aalto　　　　　　　　　　(1898–1976)
Architect

Mikael Agricola　　　　　　　　(ca. 1510–1557)
Bishop and translator

Tarja Halonen　　　　　　　　　(1943–)
President

Tove Jansson　　　　　　　　　(1914–2001)
Children's writer

Urho Kaleva Kekkonen　　　　　(1900–1986)
President

Carl Gustaf Emil Mannerheim　(1867–1951)
Military commander and poliltician

Eliel Saarinen　　　　　　　　　(1910–1961)
Architect

Jean Sibelius　　　　　　　　　(1865–1957)
Composer

Frans Eemil Sillanpää　　　　　(1888–1964)
Nobel Prize–winning author

To Find Out More

Nonfiction Books

▶ Beach, Hugh. *A Year in Lapland: Guest of the Reindeer Herders*. Seattle: University of Washington Press, 2001.

▶ Figari, Franco. *Finland: The Land of Lakes*. Milan, Italy: White Star, 2007.

▶ Robinson, Deborah. *The Sami of Northern Europe*. Minneapolis: Lerner, 2002.

Fiction Books

▶ De Gerez, Toni. *Louhi, Witch of North Farm: A Story from Finland's Epic Poem, the* Kalevala. New York: Viking Kestrel, 1986.

▶ Jansson, Tove. *Tales from Moominvalley*. New York: Farrar, Straus, and Giroux, 1995.

▶ Shepard, Aaron. *The Princess Mouse: A Tale of Finland*. New York: Atheneum Books for Young Readers, 2003.

Videos

▶ *Moomin*. 4-disc collector's set. Telescreen Japan/Teleimage, 2007.

▶ *Seven Days: Finland*. Global Television/Arcadia Films, 2007.

Web Sites

▶ **Finland Travel Guide**
www.finland.com
To find out where to go and what to do in Finland.

▶ **Finnish Government**
www.vn.fi/etusivu/en.jsp
To read about activities of the Finnish government.

▶ **The History of Finland**
www.history-of-finland.com
For a timeline of historical events and lots of links about famous Finns.

▶ **Santa Television**
www.santatelevision.com
For information about Lapland and to watch video of the northern lights.

▶ **Statistics Finland**
http://www.stat.fi/index_en.html
For loads of statistics on Finland.

▶ **Virtual Finland**
www.virtual.finland.fi
For a wealth of information about Finnish society, culture, and history.

▶ **The World Factbook: Finland**
www.cia.gov/library/publications/
the-world-factbook/geos/fi.html
To find basic information and statistics on Finland.

Organizations and Embassies

▶ **Embassy of Finland**
3301 Massachusetts Avenue, NW
Washington, DC 20008
202-298-5800
www.finland.org/en

▶ **Embassy of Finland in Canada**
55 Metcalfe Street, Suite 850
Ottawa, Ontario K1P 6L5
Canada
613-288-2244
www.finland.ca/en/

Index

Page numbers in *italics* indicate illustrations.

Meet the Author

GERI CLARK was born and raised outside New York City and has always had an itch to travel and meet new people. She's also always loved writing and animals. After graduating from Cornell University with a degree in biology and from New York University with a degree in journalism (two things that might not seem to go together), she was lucky enough to have some jobs early in her career that forced her to travel across the United States. She was the "animal and bug producer" on a science news show for ABC News, a job that combined lots of travel, animals, and writing. Although she is an avid traveler, this is Clark's first book about a foreign place. Most of her past work has focused on science, nature, and medicine.

Clark is now a freelance writer living in Connecticut with her husband, her son, and a houseful of animals. She travels as much as she can and takes pride in the fact that her young son loves to pack his own suitcase and knows how to get through airport screening.

Photo Credits